SOUTHERN OREGON BEER

A Pioneering History

PHIL BUSSE

Foreword by Jim Mills, Founder, Caldera Brewing Company

AMERICAN PALATE

Published by American Palate
A Division of The History Press
Charleston, SC
www.historypress.com

Copyright © 2019 by Phil Busse
All rights reserved

Cover image: Crater Lake. Photographs in the Carol M. Highsmith Archive, Library of Congress, Prints and Photographs Division.

First published 2019

Manufactured in the United States

ISBN 9781467142441

Library of Congress Control Number: 2019936994

Notice: The information in this book is true and complete to the best of our knowledge. It is offered without guarantee on the part of the author or The History Press. The author and The History Press disclaim all liability in connection with the use of this book.

All rights reserved. No part of this book may be reproduced or transmitted in any form whatsoever without prior written permission from the publisher except in the case of brief quotations embodied in critical articles and reviews.

To Hans Kessler, the first true brewmeister I knew.

CONTENTS

Foreword, by Jim Mills   7
Preface   9
Acknowledgements   15

1. 1851–1884, Gold Rushes, German Immigrants and Lagers   19
2. 1884–1908, Railroads and Pioneer Women   38
3. 1908–1934, End of an Era: Prohibition!   48
4. 1880s–1950s, Hops Keep an Industry Afloat   59
5. 1933–1996, Prohibition Ends, Homebrew Clubs and Brewpubs   67
6. 1996–2014, After the Flood, The Next Chapter Begins   85
7. Now and Beyond?   98

Appendix. Current Southern Oregon Breweries   107

Bibliography   109
About the Author   112

FOREWORD

It all started in a small, dark basement closet. The sweet smell of fermenting wort was in the air. My cousin Rick was fermenting another batch of his dark, strong Amber Ale. His home brew was about 7.5 percent alcohol by volume and was hopped with a spicy noble hop. I recall the heavy malt flavors with a spicy hop finish. It was 1980, and I took a sip from my cousin Rick's homebrew and was completely blown away by the flavors! President Jimmy Carter had just legalized homebrewing the year before. I had always had sips of my dad's beers, usually Coors and Henry Weinhard's Private Reserve. I had never tasted a true homebrew before. This experience put me on a course of everything beer for the rest of my life.

In 1981, I began collecting beer bottles and cans, mostly imported beers at the time. My extended family would always bring me bottles and cans back from their travels to Africa and Europe. My Aunt Jean even smuggled out a bottle from East Germany before the wall came down. Fast forward to the present day, and I now have over seven thousand bottles and cans in my collection on display at the Caldera Brewery & Restaurant in Ashland—the largest beer bottle and can collection in Oregon.

I started homebrewing when I was nineteen years old. When I was twenty-one years old, I got a job at Rogue Ales in Ashland bartending and working in the kitchen. I had a desire to learn how to brew commercially, so I started washing kegs for free for a chance to work in the brewery. Eventually, I was hired on as brewer's assistant. In 1995, I was hired on as head brewer at the Ashland location while working on my business plan to start Caldera Brewing Company.

Foreword

I started Caldera in 1997, with the first brew landing on the Fourth of July. For the first six years, I self-distributed my beers around Southern Oregon and ultimately to bars and restaurants in Eugene and Portland. Oh, the abuse my poor Subaru took delivering kegs, with two hatchback windows replaced! The original concept of Caldera was draft only, without a pub or taproom. However, things change, and the beer landscape was ready for Caldera package beers. For the first eight years, Caldera was draft (keg) only until June 2005, when the Pale Ale was put into cans. Caldera was the first craft brewery on the West Coast to brew and can its own beer. People thought I was crazy to put craft beer in a can, but I knew of all the benefits going into this venture. The only downside was educating consumers that good beer could actually come from a can. More than two decades after helping pioneer craft beer in cans, it is an industry standard.

I am thrilled to be a part of Southern Oregon beer history. I have been brewing beer professionally for over twenty-five years and am not only excited about the next challenges but also am proud to be part of this generation of craft brewers.

—Jim Mills, Proprietor and Head Brewer
CalderaBrewing.com

PREFACE

When I was contacted to consider writing a book about the "beer history of Southern Oregon," at first, I dismissed the idea. It seemed like a gimmick. Like someone posting a sign that says "free beer" to attract attention.

But my contact at The History Press, Laurie Krill, advised me that they were not looking for a tourist guide or a review of beers, but something that gave insights into what makes the region interesting and different—and, more precisely, that beer can be a portal through which a region may be considered for all of its qualities and quirks. It was good advice, and indeed, that is true. During months of research, I discovered that beer is a wide-angle lens through which history can be considered. (And, no, I don't mean "beer googles.") This is not "drunk history," although there are certainly rowdy stories about German brass bands marching down the streets of Jacksonville toward a massive three-story brewery, and there are tales about beer sold by the bucket full for a quarter by a woman in Grants Pass who kept parrots on her shoulders. But the real heft and thrust of this book is about how beer, brewers and breweries can identify the big changes and themes in the past 150 years of Southern Oregon's history, about how these men, women and institutions are important markers and metrics for how history is forming and changing.

For example, the story begins in Jacksonville when gold was discovered in 1851. That is a common starting point for modern history in Southern Oregon. But what makes breweries interesting and important to this story

Preface

is that when the first brewery is opened five years later, in 1856, it was a marker that Jacksonville had matured from an overnight boomtown to a city that planned to stay around; the arrival of a brewery was a turning point for the city.

Consider that in the 1850s resources were so scarce and Jacksonville was so isolated that it cost one dollar to mail a letter and to buy a pound of flour (about twenty-six dollars in current value). To construct a brewery was nothing short of building a space station on the moon. There is no way that a sane person would spend the piles of money and effort to drag cooper kettles and tanks over hundreds of bumpy mountain passes and to track down and import resources like wheat, barley and hops, if there wasn't good potential that Jacksonville would be around for a few years to return on that investment.

Writing this book helped me connect a number of dots, about the role of German immigrants in the mid-nineteenth century; about the function of railroads to the development of the West; about the differences between ales and lagers; and about how a few small changes in laws uncorked massive changes in the beer industry—first, the federal legalization of homebrewing in 1978 and then the legislation permitting brewpubs in Oregon in 1985.

I was particularly interested in many of these ideas, as my childhood was spent in Wisconsin during the 1970s and '80s, both a wonderful and a horrible time for beer, and one in which beer was locked down by companies like Schlitz and Miller, both then located in Milwaukee and together controlling half of the entire market. Heck, it is near impossible to grow up in Wisconsin and not have some sense of the beer industry osmosis into your brain. After all, the state's baseball team is named for the profession of beer brewing, and during my formative years, the most-watched TV show in America was *Laverne & Shirley*, a show set in Milwaukee with two smart-mouthed roommates working on the assembly line at Shotz Brewery, an easy stand-in for Schlitz. I distinctly remember riding in the back seat of my parents' blue station wagon as we drove to my grandparents' house near Milwaukee and the biting smell of yeast hanging like a cloud over the highway.

What I did not realize until researching and writing this book, though, was how the history of those breweries ties into a mass immigration of Germans in the mid-nineteenth century—the so-called 48ers who primarily settled into Midwest cities like Milwaukee and St. Louis but also ventured into boomtowns like Jacksonville, Oregon and Golden, Colorado, often on the heels of a gold rush, but who stuck around to set up breweries. Those German immigrants dramatically changed American culture, bringing

Preface

kindergarten and Christmas trees, and also shifting the country's drinking habits from whiskey and ciders to predominately beer—and, more precisely, lagers. Southern Oregon was not removed from these cultural changes, and through my research, it was exhilarating to be introduced across the centuries to a number of these German immigrants, like tough-guy Veit Schutz, who set up the largest brewery in nineteenth-century Jacksonville, a hulking three-story structure that included underground caves for cooling, indoor waterwheels and a second-floor gym and dance hall, and Joseph Wetterer, who set up a competing brewery in Jacksonville, and his wife, Fredericka Wetterer, who outlived him and was the first woman to own a brewery in Oregon. Leafing through a set of meticulous receipts she kept—purchases from Henry Weinhard (not just the company, but handwritten receipts from the very man) and receipts for hops deliveries from Roseburg—truly provided the details that helped reconstruct what life was like for a pioneer in nineteenth-century Oregon and brought to me the reality of these towns and breweries.

For most of my professional career, I have worked as a journalist, writing for publications like *San Francisco Weekly*, *Eugene Weekly*, *Bend Source* and the *Portland Mercury*. Five years ago, I launched the *Rogue Valley Messenger*, a biweekly publication that distributes from Ashland to Grants Pass. As the publisher and editor, I have my choice of which articles I want to write and also play the role of backstop—that is, writing articles when no one wants to do so or when a writer fumbles an assignment. For all of these reasons, I have been lucky enough and responsible for writing dozens of reviews about beers from Southern Oregon's breweries. Those served as a preface for this book.

But this is not a book that reviews various beer styles and flavors from the dozens of breweries in Southern Oregon (although I will happily share my opinions about the many fine beers in the area, if you ask). No, instead, I structured this book around larger themes—about the impact of German immigration; about pioneer women's role as survivors and entrepreneurs; and about local, independent businesses versus corporate giants intent on consolidating the national market. Within the outlines of those themes, Southern Oregon provides important and intriguing case studies.

For example, because Southern Oregon was one of the later regions in America to be connected by railroads, it was, at first, immune to many of the pressures of a national market consolidating in the later nineteenth century. Anheuser-Busch pioneered refrigerated railcars to expand its Budweiser empire and, in the process, helped wipe out hundreds of local

Preface

breweries at the turn of the twentieth century (years before Prohibition finished the job). The isolation of the region has shaped—and continues to do so—opportunities for Southern Oregon breweries and also provides business models different from the prevailing conversations.

Also, Southern Oregon provides specific examples about how western towns in the nineteenth century often provided a wider and more interesting horizon of opportunities than their more established eastern counterparts. Places like Grants Pass needed whatever talent and resources were available and, as such, often—or, at least, sometimes—provided chances for entrepreneurs that eastern cities may note have, regardless of class, race and gender.

Consider that in the later nineteenth century, nearly half of the breweries in Southern Oregon were owned by women, a completely abnormal statistic from the rest of the country. Perhaps one of the most intriguing "characters" in this book is Marie Kienlen, who pops up again and again throughout the story. A flamboyant Frenchwoman, Kienlen is possibly the first woman brewer in Oregon, and she ran a bustling brewery for more than a decade in Grants Pass's business district. (Yup, Kienlen's the one who had parrots on her shoulders, and she erected the brick building that today houses Climate City Brewery.) But although Kienlen was popular with the city's working class, she was at odds with the stodgy all-male city council who were determined to shut down alcohol drinking, even if it meant that the city's streets would not be paved for another few years with the loss of tax revenue. This conflict is particularly interesting because the prevailing theory is that Prohibition happened in large part because women received the right to vote and ultimately voted in large numbers for Prohibition. But in Grants Pass, the reverse was true—or at least it is a different, more nuanced story than what is popularly told.

Southern Oregon breweries also hold a peculiar and important countertrend to contemporary industry and historical trends. Certainly, Caldera Brewing in Ashland has emerged as a powerhouse, but even that brewery remains much more congenial than corporate and, like other breweries in the region, holds principles about community building and environmental stewardship over profits.

I finished this book with a good sense of pride and optimism about what Southern Oregon breweries are doing and what contributions they can bring to the industry at large. They are not simply cookie-cutter operations but independent and ethical and seem to earnestly be trying to maintain breweries and the craft beer business as something unique and personal.

Preface

If breweries are not trying to change the world at large, they are certainly striving to create friendly and fun communities close by.

Moreover, in writing the book, I also gained more pride for the region's beer industry—and its importance. Often, the breweries in Portland and Bend are cited as the shining examples for how important beer is for the state of Oregon, with Southern Oregon as an afterthought. Yes, most of the big producers are located in those cities, although Caldera certainly has an important presence in the state. But, by the numbers, there are nearly the same concentration of breweries—roughly two dozen in Southern Oregon, compared with thirty or so in Central Oregon and, per capita, nearly equal to Portland. I touch on these themes lightly in the final chapter, but they are worthwhile announcing here more plainly: I have written about breweries throughout the state of Oregon, and there is truly something special about the ones in Southern Oregon. In the nineteenth century, they announced the arrival of a new town—and they were intent on becoming a hub for those new communities, like Veit Schutz's City Brewery in Jacksonville, which hosted fitness and fencing classes for its patrons, and John and Mary Mehl's brewery on the coast, which gave out free beer after each fire in town. (There was no shortage of fires during those decades, including several that burned down breweries.) Those intents for community building still exist today with breweries like Walkabout in Medford hosting yoga classes, Standing Stone Brewery in Ashland committing to sustainability and several breweries in the region linking up to host chummy, but competitive, hockey and bowling leagues. There truly was something unique about the nineteenth-century breweries in Jacksonville and Grants Pass, and that something special has reemerged in the twenty-first century throughout the region.

One additional heads-up as you read this book: I took all measures to check and confirm various facts and dates peppered throughout the book. But that was not always easy. I had wonderful help from Kira Lesley at the Southern Oregon Historical Society and from several other local historians and records. However, there are large gaps in historical records, and those records that do exist sometimes tell different "facts" and stories from one another.

For example, no one and no single historical record was able to definitively pin down the date that Veit Schutz opened his City Brewery in Jacksonville. Official records from a registry of businesses list Schutz opening the City Brewery in 1869, but that is almost certainly incorrect, as there are records from Schutz advertising in local newspapers several

Preface

years before then. A recently erected placard near the site of the brewery's caves notes the opening as 1860, while other historic records indicate a time closer to 1856.

Even Schutz's age was difficult to pin down. A brochure from his funeral lists his age as "about 72 years," and various other records list his birthyear as 1820, 1823 or 1827.

Such discrepancies can be frustrating in search for the absolute truth, but they can be fun mysteries to try to unravel—and where appropriate I explain the different sources of information and what their implications may be. Sorting through these facts and playing detective were the most intriguing parts of putting together this book—and I hope that my research and conjectures provide insights to the lore and potential different realities that the various facts spell out. Even for a history book, it seems as if the pursuit of these facts can be as interesting, insightful and important as the facts themselves.

ACKNOWLEDGEMENTS

This book spans more than 150 years of history, as pulled from newspaper articles, photographs, historic notes and contemporary interviews. In the process of researching the book, I was amazed by the generosity of so many people.

The book would not be possible without the research and resources from the Southern Oregon Historical Society (SOHS) in downtown Medford. It was such a joy to meet the staff there, and in particular, Kira Lesley provided me with enthused attention and folders full of the puzzle pieces that added up to stories and people in this book. My first request for information was a simple email that included a couple names—Veit Schutz and Joseph Wetterer. At the time, I knew little more than that these two men started breweries in Jacksonville in the mid-nineteenth century. When I arrived at SOHS, there were several manila folders waiting for me, filled with photographs, newspaper articles about the brewers and even hand-drawn sketches for the plans for Schutz's City Brewery. The staff at SOHS shared my curiosity and excitement about the project and even let me work past closing time, which was greatly appreciated.

Moreover, when SOHS did not have specific information, they helped me find it with other local historians. I was surprised to receive a lengthy email one Friday evening from Larry Mullaly, who had been told that I was interested in the history of the Oregon & California Railroad. With no prompting, he provided me all of his notes from a detailed presentation he had done a few years earlier. I also am duly impressed by Ben Truwe, who

Acknowledgements

has archived thousands of historical Medford-area newspapers; his database provided me with information to re-create the day-by-day operations from Southern Oregon Brewery at the turn of the twentieth century.

I also appreciated the support from Historic Jacksonville Inc. Carolyn Kingsnorth has posted a collection of wonderful stories on various inhabitants from the early years in Jacksonville and took time from her schedule to give me a personalized walking tour of the town. Help like that allowed me to understand what life was like in Jacksonville in the 1850s and '60s, when the region's first breweries set up shop. I also appreciated another local historian, Larry Smith, who responded to an email request within minutes with a phone call, even though he was on vacation. Enthusiasm like that for local history was the fuel for writing this book.

Likewise, the women at the Josephine County Historical Library greeted me like a long-lost relative and helped me leaf through the folders there—and provided me with my favorite photograph in the book, a rare picture of Marie Kienlen holding parrots. She was a character, and this picture is truly worth more than a thousand words.

The brewers in Southern Oregon were also kind and excited to share information—Jim Mills with Caldera, Cameron Litton with Walkabout, Nick Ellis with Opposition and Tessa Delaney with Portal all generously gave me time, information, photographs and plenty of beer samples.

I first met Hubert Smith as the author for a long and detailed article about beer brewing in Jacksonville, Oregon. That article sparked my interest in the "characters" who first brewed beer in the region and helped set me on the right course. Later, I met Hubert in person and was charmed. He had been the first brewer for Wild River Pizza in 1990 and told me about how he matured from a homebrewer to a commercial one—and an award-winning one at that. When talking, he held no punches and told a story that encompassed not just his experiences but an entire nationwide movement to return to classic beers.

Likewise, Tiah Edmunson-Morton of Oregon State University was a person whom I first "met" through her writing. She maintains an enthusiastic and well-informed blog (TheBrewstorian), and those entries opened my eyes to the importance of the hops industry in Oregon. We had such a fun interview on the OSU campus. We talked for a couple hours about people like Fredericka Wetterer, and Tiah shared her notes and folders of receipts she had gathered on this pioneer woman. It was as if we were talking about an old friend.

Acknowledgements

My longtime friend Matt Martin has been supportive of my many projects, and I appreciate that he lent me his camera so that the contemporary photos in this book were not taken on my iPhone, and a newer friend Andrew Robison was nice enough to clear out his Airbnb rental in Medford for me each time I traveled to the region for interviews and research. It helped make writing this book so much more affordable—and fun! Also, thanks to Nick Blakeslee, who provided a number of the photos in this book. As the beer reviewer for the *Rogue Valley Messenger*, Nick is constantly discovering new places and happy to share them.

And, most of all, my wife, Katie, who took over most of the early morning duties of childcare so that I could stay up late writing (and, consequently, sleep in the next day). And, although a wine drinker herself, she also listened to me prattle on about the differences between ales and lagers and why they historically mattered and about the various characters of the book as they came into focus for me. It is not always fun being at ground zero for a creative process, but she encouraged me to write this book and supported me through the entire process.

All told, I thoroughly enjoyed researching this book because of the people I met along the way—yes, the brewers from the nineteenth century and the pioneers who moved into Southern Oregon, but more so the dozens of people in Southern Oregon today for whom beer is clearly an important hub for their communities and who were happy to share.

1
1851–1884

Gold Rushes, German Immigrants and Lagers

When Veit Schutz arrived in Jacksonville, Oregon, in 1853, the town was already an overnight sensation, percolating with excitement and expectation. Nestled at the base of Miller Mountain, a small stream rolls into the valley and gold had been discovered collecting around the river rock two years earlier.

Noticeably short, standing not more than five feet tall, with a broad forehead and trim mustache, Schutz was, if nothing else, determined. The *Southern Oregon Pioneer Association Records* remarks that Schutz quickly earned a reputation as a "nervy little fellow [who] knew no fear." That same report also notes that the German quickly picked up the nickname "Lil' Schutz," although it hastens to point out no one called him that directly to his face. The report also likens him to a "bantam roster."

A year shy of thirty, and like a growing wave of German immigrants into America, he carried with him a youthful zeal for adventure and an equal sense of civic purpose. Unlike immigrants from other countries, such as the thousands fleeing famine in Ireland, many Germans were arriving in American cities and towns with wealth, education, a hunger for social change and a thirst for lagers—not to mention the know-how to brew them. Born in Bavaria in 1823, Schutz had begun brewing at the age of thirteen.

But Schutz wasn't in Jacksonville to brew beer—at least, not yet. He was there for the gold rush. According to his application for American citizenship, Schutz had arrived in America in 1850—not coincidentally the year after the California gold rush kicked off and, also not coincidentally, on the heels of a failed social revolution in Germany that was pushing tens of thousands of young, idealistic men and women from their homeland. Like the other so-called 48ers leaving Germany (not to be confused with the 49ers flocking to California), Schutz had arrived in America as part of one of the most significant migrations in world history—and one that hit America like a meteoroid, shifting the young country from its cultural axis. During the 1850s, over one million Germans arrived in America, the bulk settling in the newly forming midwestern cities of Milwaukee, Cincinnati and St. Louis, as well as a sizable population in the new state of Texas and thousands of others sprinkled throughout western boomtowns like Golden, Colorado, and Jacksonville, Oregon. Having failed in their social revolution, they approached their new lives with the fervor of a born-again. With the calculation and determination of people who have lost once before and are determined not to do so again, they went about the business of setting up their comeback, establishing new utopias with their own ideals of community service, public enterprise and, yes, beer gardens. Many were instrumental in bolstering the abolitionist movement and building up the nascent Republican Party as it went about the serious task of dismantling slavery. Others set up newspapers, labor unions and, in Watertown, Wisconsin, just outside of Milwaukee, America's first kindergarten.

One of the most sizable and measurable impacts on American culture, though, was beer. When the 48ers and German immigrants first began arriving, most Americans drank whiskey and cider. In the mid-nineteenth century, Americans were drinking a staggering seven gallons of hard liquor (mostly whiskey) each year, as compared to current rates at two gallons. Cheaper and more plentiful than beer, whiskey was king—even a common replacement for water, which often was drawn from silty rivers and more often consider something for the livestock. There were fourteen thousand distilleries in America at the time—thirty times as many as the number of breweries. Cider and pear brandy were even more popular—and cheaper—than beer.

Beer consumption was a distant thought for most Americans, and when they did consider beer, it was almost entirely British-style ales and porters, which, at the time, had fundamental shortcomings for mass production. Primarily, ales demanded scientific precision and tools—and were notoriously unpredictable. Ales in the early and mid-nineteenth century in America were often muddy and, once tapped, soured quickly. They were, to say, not widely appealing.

A Pioneering History

With the quickness of a summer thunderstorm, though, the mass arrival of Germans—and their lagers—in the mid-nineteenth century radically and indelibly changed American drinking habits. Meaning "to store" or "to rest," lagers were more forgiving to produce and presented a much cleaner-tasting and looking beverage. During those years, German immigrants with names like Frederick Pabst, Adolphus Busch, Frederick Miller, Mathias Leinenkugel, Valentin Blatz, Eberhard Anheuser, Joseph Schlitz and Adolph Kohrs (Coors) arrived in America and set up breweries in their newly adopted towns and cities. In 1850, there were only 431 commercial breweries in the entire country; over the next two decades, that number grew tenfold.

In 1852, the same year Schutz first arrived in Oregon and a year before he first stepped into Jacksonville, another German immigrant, Henry Saxer, opened Liberty Brewery in Portland, the first brewery in Oregon. Four years later, the same year that the first brewery opened in Jacksonville, another German, Henry Weinhard, first visited Portland and would soon give his name to Oregon's most enduring brewery.

The change was massive. By the 1890s, the volume of beer an average American man drank each year had nearly quadrupled to thirty-six gallons from just ten gallons twenty years prior. Late nineteenth-century census data show that while German immigrants accounted for roughly 10 percent of America's workforce, over 80 percent of all working brewers in America were immigrants from Germany, not to mention 45 percent of saloon keepers and one-third of all bartenders. (Not completely incidental, German immigrants were also 75 percent of all pork butchers and sausage makers in America at that time.)

In Jacksonville, one-tenth of the growing population was German-born, and moreover, one-third of the town reportedly spoke German, a language that also encompassed emigrants from adjacent countries like Austria and Switzerland. Nor was Schutz the only German to arrive in Southern Oregon with brewing experience. In the fall of 1856, four years after Schutz's arrival, another brewer, from Baden, Joseph Wetterer, moved to town and set off a crosstown, decades-long rivalry of breweries.

By 1856, Jacksonville had settled into a crude sense of civilization, even with flashes of urbane sophistication. In the first year after the gold rush began, there was the first murder: a miner shot dead by a "gambler named Brown," according to an 1884 book, *History: Southern Oregon*. Without an established court, a group of men hastily convened an ad hoc court in which "Brown was tried by the rules of right and wrong." Not surprisingly, he was "clearly proved guilty of a cowardly murder, and taken to an oak grove, hanged, and buried under a tree." The account goes on to point out that "the remains have never been removed." By the next year, though, a U.S. District judge was appointed to the region, and Jacksonville began to take on the infrastructure of a proper city.

As Jacksonville was far removed from any other town, delivery routes were set up. A rider, Cornelius Beekman, zipped across the border with California a few times each week. Carrying letters for $1 a pop and gold dust for 5 percent of its value, he quickly amassed a tidy fortune and, by 1857, established the main bank in town. In a report published in 1903, after all the Wild West dust had settled, it is estimated that during the town's two or three halcyon decades, roughly $40 million in gold traveled across the countertops at Beekman's bank—an amount equivalent to more than $1 billion in current value.

In the first few years, the main road through town, California Street, was pounded dirt, lined on either side with makeshift log houses and pitched canvas tents that functioned as general stores and pop-up saloons serving throat-scorching whiskey and apple brandies. But one by one, the tents were replaced with an elegant collection of one- and two-story brick buildings lining the wide main street. On the corner of California and Oregon Streets—the epicenter for the new town—was El Dorado Saloon, a lively block-long tavern. Around the corner stood Palmetto Bowling Saloon and the Table Rock Saloon, which doubled as a curiosity museum holding fossils, the first piece of gold discovered in town, the territory's first billiard table and even a piece of a rope used in a hanging.

With 3,000 mostly permanent residents, Jacksonville bustled with one of the largest populations in the Oregon Territory—and perhaps the most diverse. (By comparison, although Portland also grew quickly in the subsequent decade, it started the 1860s with a population of 2,874.) On the second floor above Table Rock Saloon was a part-time synagogue, and across the street was a meeting space for one of the town's two Red Man Society groups, a fraternal order that dates back to the Tea Party. Two branches formed in Jacksonville: one that spoke German, the other English. Jacksonville became home to Oregon's first Chinatown, a two-block-long collection of tents, shacks and a brothel that still stands today but now houses the town's fire department. By the 1870 census for Jackson County, there were 4,778 persons counted in the region. Of these, 634 were Chinese, roughly equal to the German-born population. Although the Chinese were not legally allowed to hold leases or contracts, several men amassed sizable fortunes, including Gin Lin, who reportedly held in

A Pioneering History

Beekman's bank $1 million earned from working the mines and river banks. He arrived in town now and again with one of his four wives in a buggy pulled by a high-stepping horse.

Likewise, Schutz tried to figure out how to make his money. Even as hundreds of men flocked to the boomtown, Jacksonville remained isolated, locked in by the thick forests and steep mountains. To the north, the Oregon Trail had deposited tens of thousands of pioneers, but those families had settled 150 miles north in the lush Willamette Valley, a relatively flat expanse flanked at its southern reaches by treacherous canyons and mountains that keep most from wandering too far south. Likewise, entry to the south is blocked at the border between California and the Oregon Territory by the Siskiyou Mountains, which stand like a fortress wall; only small trickles of footpaths trace through the mountain passes—and these vanished under feet of snow for half of the year. By 1851, the year of gold discovery in Jacksonville, only twenty-seven European settlers were making their homes in the area.

Veit Schutz as a young man, a "bantam rooster" from Germany and one of Oregon's first brewers. *SOHS #01691.*

It was this mix of isolation and optimism, though, that provided an opportunity for Schutz. As much as the gold dust and nuggets, the supplies necessary to keep one alive were equally valuable. Quite literally, in 1852, flour and salt were worth their weight in gold in Jacksonville. With the nearest farm one hundred miles removed and no reliable supply distribution yet, the town's first winter was so bleak that most inhabitants simply lived off gamey deer meat—no salt.

During his first year there, Schutz reportedly set up a dry goods store in Jacksonville. A year later, though, presumably bored by the stay-home tranquility of managing a retail store, he shifted his role in the distribution chain to one more electric with adventure and danger. When the snow melted in 1853, he teamed up with Peter Britt, who had shown up in Jacksonville roughly the same time as Schutz, lugging with him three hundred pounds of photographic equipment. Although not directly from Germany, Britt was Swiss-German and had crossed the American continent with three other men from Switzerland, two of whom had ditched him—and his onerous load of photographic equipment—along the way. Schutz and Britt decided to team up and invest in a "mule pack train." It was the first method of delivering goods into Jacksonville from the port town of Crescent City, one hundred miles southwest in California.

But the value of "mule packing" was in its direct relationship to danger. Two years after Britt and Schutz started their business, a driver and one of their mules were shot while Schutz was crossing back into Jacksonville. Reportedly, Schutz tried to give chase into the bush, but the others restrained him, recognizing his pursuit as a suicide mission.

Joseph Wetterer, soon to be Schutz's rival in a crosstown brewery, arrived in Jacksonville under very different circumstances—and apparently with a different disposition from Schutz. According to articles written many decades later by his son in the *Oregon Journal*, the elder Wetterer had mined in California for three years after leaving Germany—and had accumulated a modest fortune. But by the early 1850s, most of the claims in Central California had been snatched up or given way to industrialized hydraulic mining; the notion of a lone, gold-panning miner was already dated. Many miners, like Wetterer, pushed north, prospecting new opportunities. In a series of "recollection" columns in the early 1930s, Wetterer's son writes that his dad arrived in Jacksonville in 1853.

Like many historical notes, though, those dates are a bit fuzzy. (Consider that the birth year for Wetterer's rival, Schutz, is listed as 1820, 1823 and 1827, depending on the source, and his obituary lists his age as "about 72 years.") Depending on which report and historical source, Wetterer opened a brewery either a year or three after arriving in Jacksonville—or even as many as six years later.

An obituary states that Wetterer emigrated from Germany in 1848, which, if true, places him in the elite company of the original 48ers departing from Germany after their failed revolution. The obituary also states that Wetterer arrived in Jacksonville in the fall of 1856, three years later than his son claims, and that Wetterer started the Eagle Brewery in 1857. The facts and dates in his obituary are certainly more contemporaneous than recollections decades later, and they also better align with what is known about Wetterer's constitution as a hardworking and diligent German. Otherwise, what was Wetterer doing for those several years between arriving in town in 1853, as his son claims, and starting a brewery in 1859, another date often noted as the opening of the Eagle Brewery?

But perhaps those facts also are nitpicking. The upshot is the same: In the 1850s, Wetterer and Schutz arrived in an Oregon gold rush boomtown, two

A Pioneering History

Germans with the knowledge of how to brew beer and puzzle pieces to a larger picture that was shaping up across America.

What is clear is that a brewery opened in Jacksonville during the town's first rowdy years—some records note 1852, some pick 1853, others say 1856. Some records and accounts at the Southern Oregon Historical Society place the opening of the first brewery in Jacksonville at 1852, while others state 1856. The difference is critical because the earlier date would rival the opening of the Liberty Brewery in Portland and potentially place Oregon's first brewery in Southern Oregon, as opposed to Portland. Yet it is highly unlikely that someone would have been able—or crazy or ambitious enough—to open a brewery in Jacksonville in 1852, one year after the town began to take shape. At that time, supplies were so remote that a freshly baked loaf of bread was a luxury more valuable than its weight in gold, with both yeast and wheat rare. More likely, the building that housed the first brewery was erected in 1852, and four years later, once the town was more settled and supplies more readily available, the first brewery opened.

What is important is that, unlike the dozen-plus saloons in Jacksonville's early years, a brewery is a very different and distinct social indicator—one that measures not only thirst and prosperity but also a belief in the town's stability and future. Given the expense and trouble to set up a brewery, a proprietor had to believe that the town would not vanish overnight and waste away all his investments. If delivering a letter or a pound of flour was worth one dollar (roughly twenty-six in current value) to Jacksonville residents, consider the investment to drag brewing tanks across the rough terrain of Southern Oregon—a task that Schutz reportedly did a few years later by shipping a copper tank from Germany. And, if wheat for bread was hard to come by, hops were even more scarce, with only eight pounds reportedly grown in the Oregon Territory in 1850.

Located catty-corner to the El Dorado Saloon, the first brewery took on the patriotic name of Eagle Brewery. There are few—if any—existing notes or records about the endeavor. Registered to J.J. Holman—apparently an Englishman—the exact details of this first Eagle Brewery and J.J. Holman vanished like ghosts into history. Soon after opening, Holman sold the brewery to the German brewer Wetterer, who moved the equipment and facility two hundred yards up a small hill to 355 South Oregon Street. Still standing today, the building is a plain and straightforward affair: an A-frame pop-up structure that looks like a Monopoly game piece. Inside, though, was old-world charm and functionality. A brick-lined basement cellar is a cool, dry storage area for the lagers, and the main room is lined with a dark

Joseph Wetterer stands on the porch of the Eagle Brewery, circa 1856. *SOHS #21077.*

wood bar, mirrors and painted murals. Wetterer also added a beer garden typical to breweries in Germany, and in 1859, the same year that Oregon was admitted to the union, he plotted his home adjacent to the brewery. A year later, he married his wife, Fredericka, another German American, whose sister, coincidentally, was married to another brewer in Roseburg.

Conversely—and fitting to his character—Schutz's story and timeline for launching his brewery are more ambiguous and ambitious than Wetterer's. Schutz most certainly was a member of the German brass band in town, playing the booming bass drum, and he stepped into public service as the county coroner. Likewise, when he finally built a brewery, he did so in grand fashion—and with a similar sense of bravado and public purpose, setting a wood-frame, three-story barn-like structure at the far reaches of California Street, an ideal location adjacent to the Jackson Creek Mining operations. The structure was set down a sloping hillside from his friend and former business partner Peter Britt's home and extensive garden. The brewery was one of the largest and tallest buildings in town at the time, and on the second floor, Schutz built a gymnasium for his fellow Germans, an open room with medicine balls, pommel horses and fencing foils that doubled as a hall for masquerade balls and weddings and even reportedly as a roller rink.

A Pioneering History

Veit Schutz's City Brewery in Jacksonville, operational from 1856 to 1892. The second floor held a gymnasium. *SOHS #02937.*

Like beer gardens in Germany, many of the German breweries opened in late nineteenth-century America did so with an underlying philosophy about public betterment. So-called turnvereins, or the Americanized "Turner Halls" were community centers for progressive politics and fitness, with men fencing, doing gymnastics and tumbling, often dressed in bleach white head-to-toe uniforms. Prevalent in American towns in the second half of the nineteenth century, Turner Halls claimed a membership topping one million. Schutz opened a "Turner" society in Jacksonville in 1863, and his brewery's second floor served as the meeting space, modestly called Veit Schutz Hall.

The actual brewing happened on the building's first floor. With electricity not arriving in Jacksonville until a half-century later, Schutz ingeniously designed a reservoir at the back side of the structure; from here, a flume pushed the water through the first floor and spun a waterwheel to supply hundreds of gallons of fresh water. The whole structure itself was built into the sloping hillside, with caves and caverns providing natural cooling storage areas, necessary to maintain cool and stable temperatures for lagers, especially important in Southern Oregon's dry, hot summers. It is likely Schutz was producing more than two hundred barrels each year, an impressive volume

Men drinking on the Britt gardens/City Brewery, keg in foreground. *SOHS #00763*.

for a city with three thousand residents and a second brewery in town and considering they weren't exporting the beer out of Jacksonville, as there was nowhere or no way to ship the beer. Intriguingly, there also is evidence of a fairly ambitious bottling facility. Although there is no physical evidence remaining, a July 25, 1889 article in a local newspaper, the *Democratic Times*, reports on the collapse of a side building to the brewery, which, the article explains, was a well-known bottling facility: "Schutz and others were there at the time, but they fortunately escaped with slight bruises." The article adds, "Several dozens of the bottled beer were lost in the collapse."

But it is tricky to pinpoint when Schutz opened his extravagant City Brewery. Consider the 1889 *Democratic Times* article. It notes that the brewery was "built many years ago" and that Schutz has been bottling for "sometime past." Some historical notes indicate that he opened the City Brewery in 1856, which would predate Wetterer's Eagle Brewery by a year or two—that presumption fits into Schutz's timeline, as 1856 is the year he seems to have given up his mule packing business.

Official records from a registry of businesses, however, list Schutz opening the City Brewery in 1869, which is almost certainly incorrect, as there are records from Schutz advertising in local newspapers several years before then. On a recently erected placard near the site of the brewery's caves, Historic Jacksonville notes the opening as 1860, which is probably as accurate as it gets.

What is most likely is that Schutz simply did not register the brewery until years after it opened, a likelihood that falls into a larger picture of his personality. Not one to follow protocol, during his lifetime Schutz racked up a number of violations—for failing to license the business, even years after it had been operating; for selling to minors; and, in 1883, a three-dollar fine for refusing to register his dog. Likewise, if birds of a feather truly do flock, his friend Peter Britt, on whose property he built the three-story City Brewery and who planted the first grapevines in the region and began bottling hundreds of gallons of wine for sale, avoided paying taxes on his wine sales for years.

Schutz's City Brewery gained a reputation as varied and boisterous as the German brewer himself—seemingly well-loved, but also brusque and volatile. A popular ditty from the era memorializes evenings at the City Brewery. Written by Colonel Robert Miller, a local attorney and prominent Democrat, the song rhapsodizes: "The pleasure we had at Veit Schultz hall / the fun we had I'll n'er forget! / Nor will I ever those days regret / To make the girls laugh was our intent / Wherever they'd go, of course we went!" But in those same memoirs and historical papers that Miller's song is found appears a different assessment from an apparently more prudish resident and self-appointed historian, Fletcher Linn, who points out that the City Brewery was "not visited by the better class of young people."

Much that can be learned about Wetterer's and Schutz's breweries plays out in the local newspapers from the time. With the tone of a snake oil salesman, in an 1859 ad in the *Oregon Sentinel* (a Democrat, and decidedly and disgracefully proslavery newspaper), Wetterer addresses "those who wish to gain strength," and instructs them to "go to the Eagle Brewery." In block letters, the ad announces, "Best Lager Beer." The ad notes that the brewery would not sell less than "one bottle or quart, which is the smallest dose they can prescribe for the afflicted."

Although the ads never mention the crosstown competition by name, the rivalry continued to play out in the town's newspapers alongside the bitter political jabs of the day—mainly pertaining to the ongoing Civil War ripping apart the eastern half of the country and between Democrat and antislavery Republican ideals of the day. In October 1963, Wetterer ran an ad, again in the *Oregon Sentinel*, with the tone of a news flash: "The proprietor announces that the arrangements of his Brewery are so extensive and complete that he can defy all competition in Southern Oregon in making an No. 1 article of Lager Beer."

In 1864, with his brewery apparently fully operational, Schutz took out a personal ad, a not-entirely-novel approach for mating in larger cities at the time. Fifteen years past the average marrying age for the era, Schutz was decidedly middle-aged when he published his solicitation in the *Oregon Intelligencer*, another short-lived newspaper in Jacksonville. Schutz was stout and lively, but at this age, his features had hardened like a boxer: "Veit Schutz," the ad reads, "requests us to say to the marriageable ladies that he is on the marry: that he is not old, nor young, nor is he extremely ugly, or handsome; he is not rich, nor is he poor, but makes good lager, and has a comfortable and well-furnished house…that as he is desirous of marrying, he will not be very particular, so if the lady is not very old or very young, moderate size; if not handsome, not to be considered ugly, to be a good housekeeper, and not too extravagant; not to be a scold, but have fair spunk; if not rich, to have a fair portion of the spondulix [nineteenth-century slang for money]." "Yet," he adds, "this last item will be easily dispensed if the previous ones exist."

There is no direct record whether the personal ad boosted Schutz's dating life, but two years later, he married Josephine Rollman and, for a while at least, seemingly settled into a domestic lifestyle more like his crosstown rival, Wetterer. Likewise, by 1866, Jacksonville had also shed its Wild West beginnings and settled into a more rudimentary sense of elegance and civility.

A Pioneering History

By the 1870s, breweries were popping up throughout Oregon. Largely managed by German Americans, the breweries mark where commerce and prosperity were taking root in Oregon, a state more than a decade old. In Coos Bay (then called Marshfield), a popular port and midway stop for ships traveling between San Francisco and Astoria, there was Reichert & Stauff Brewery. William Reichert also opened a brewery in McMinnville, a town southwest from Portland that sits at the crossroads for many of the nearby farming communities, including a burgeoning hops industry.

Other breweries opened up along the overland routes connecting Oregon with the rest of the country. Still an arduous thirteen-day trek from San Francisco to Portland, the stagecoach line was the most complete travel route along the West Coast. A brewery opened in the quaint town of Canyonville, one of the stops along the way; today, it is probably best known as the location of the Seven Feather Casino.

Roseburg is only twenty-five miles north from Canyonville, but in the 1870s, that distance was an immense expanse. Between the two towns, the land crinkles into a series of difficult mountain passes and canyons—and travel was difficult. But to the north of Roseburg, the land flattens into the fertile Willamette Valley, and in 1872, a railway from Portland reached Roseburg. For the next decade, the railroad did not progress any further, leaving Southern Oregon as remote as any region in America.

It is here, in Roseburg, where one of the state's most ambitious and resilient breweries in the nineteenth century was founded. Started in 1861, the brewery predated the railway, and it was all Wild West, complete with a horse walking in a circle for hours each day to turn a wheel drawing water from a nearby spring and, reportedly, a man sitting in the corner playing accordion. The brewery was established by yet another German immigrant, John Gottlieb Mehl, who had immigrated to Philadelphia in 1844 and crossed the continent to Roseburg in 1849. Known as a friendly and generous man, Mehl set up the Roseburg Brewery in 1861 and, five years later, partnered with a Swiss German, John Rast, for whom the brewery is better known. After a fire consumed the first brewery in 1871, Mehl took off thirty miles north up the railway line, settling in Oakland, Oregon, where he opened another brewery. (Meanwhile, Rast stayed in Roseburg and reopened the eponymous brewery, which continued to operate until Prohibition in 1916.)

Mehl operated the Oakland Brewery for five years before pulling up stakes again. This time, he moved with his wife, Mary, toward the Oregon coast, and they set up yet another brewery in Coquille, a small town alongside a

Rast Brewery, Roseburg, circa 1890s. One of the breweries that John Mehl set up. *Oregon State University archives.*

riverway connecting the lush forests with an ocean port. At the time, the town was teaming with sawmills and producing fifteen thousand board feet of fir each day, loading at least one schooner per month to San Francisco. In 1874, Mehl set up the City Brewery in Coquille and began selling his kegs directly to the logging camps.

At four o'clock in the morning on April 5, 1874, a fire broke out in downtown Jacksonville. While much of Jacksonville's downtown buildings' exteriors were brick, the framework and roofs were wood—through the early morning, the fire moved along steadily. According to a news article in the *Liberal Republican*, "[A]lthough no wind was blowing, the dry lumber lazed so high and the flames spread so rapidly that nothing could be done." Embers fell onto the wide, sloping roof of Schutz's brewery and caught fire. The rest of the brewery was unharmed, but fire insurance records indicate the City Brewery sustained $2,000 damage (roughly $50,000 in current value). All told, there was $60,000 of damage throughout the town, of which only $17,000 was insured; Schutz's brewery was not. Moreover, a police report later that week indicates that the fire was started by an "incendiary device," and two men were arrested, one of whom the police identified in the crude terms of the time as a "mulatto."

Schutz poo-pooed the incident, yet a year later, he mortgaged the property for $1,400 in gold coin from Peter Britt; presumably, the loan was to cover his financial setback repairing the roof. It was a loan that Schutz never quite fully repaid during his lifetime and ultimately sealed the fate of the brewery.

By 1878, Wetterer was experiencing his own hardships. Two of his seven children died—one at eight months and another girl at three years—and there were indications that his finances were not stretching as far as his ambitions for social status. In *Brewed in the Pacific Northwest*, a 1991 book by Gary and Gloria Meier, the authors confirm a legend that the Sisters at St. Mary's Academy bartered the ten-dollar-per-term tuition for beer so that Josephine and Daisy Wetterer could attend the more esteemed school in town.

In the late summer, at only fifty years old, Wetterer had a premonition that he would die soon. He traveled to San Francisco and was treated for "dropsy," an ailment more contemporarily known as "edema." When he was away, someone broke into the brewery and stole $450 from a safe, a princely sum close to $10,000 in current value.

The next summer, in July 1879, Wetterer died. His obituary attributes common Germanic qualities to him, asserting he was "[m]anly and upright in all his dealings with his fellows" and "governed by the very strictest integrity."

A week after his obituary, the court published details about Wetterer's estate, a modest wealth amounting to nearly $10,000, including his house and all the brewing equipment. (Roughly $200,000 in today's money.) Along with his wife, Fredericka, he left five children, the youngest of whom was only four years old. Aside from three years in Portland working as a tailor, the youngest Wetterer lived his entire life, until 1948, at the very home where he was born. Meanwhile, and importantly, Fredericka chose to carry on with the Eagle Brewery—and is commonly credited with being the first woman brewer in Oregon. (See chapter 2.)

But it seems as if Joseph Wetterer provided a certain baseline of stability at the Eagle Brewery that was yanked out after his death. A year later, one of the brewers, Ernst Luvinowsky, was arrested for larceny from his employer; although no further details were available, the incident was perhaps related to the theft from Wetterer's safe while he traveled to San Francisco for dropsy treatments, or Luvinowsky was taking advantage of the new owner.

For unclear reasons, Fredericka briefly closed the brewery, and her father purchased the Wetterer estate—which he turned around and gifted to her. In 1881, she reopened Eagle Brewery under the name Mrs. Frederica Wetterer Brewery. She carried on with help from a "loyal" employee, William Heeley, whom she married in June 1883. Again, the brewery name changed, this time to the "William & Frederica Heeley Brewery."

But Heeley proved himself far less stable than Wetterer. He picked fights, including, according to an article in the *Oregon Sentinel*, a "small fracas" with the new brewer. In turn, the new brewer pressed charges for assault and battery; a jury, however, found Heeley not guilty.

Probably not coincidentally, though, several months later, someone broke into the brewery and poured "a lot of soft soap" into a three-hundred-gallon batch of lager, an affront so odd and specific that it seems unlikely that anyone but a brewer could be the culprit. Reporting on the incident, the *Oregon Sentinel* explains that the soap spoiled the batch of beer, and concludes the article, "What next!"

Soon after that incident, Heeley ventured from Jacksonville and into the new booming towns of Medford and Grants Pass, apparently looking to set up his own breweries.

By this time, Schutz was in his late fifties, and domestic life fit him like a scratchy nightshirt. He divorced his first wife; one account breezily explains fifteen years of marriage as "not proving a happy union, they divorced."

At age sixty, on the evening before the Fourth of July in 1883, Schutz married a second wife, Johanna Lipkey. The ceremony was conducted a few doors down from Wetterer's Eagle Brewery and, at first, was uncharacteristically (for Schutz) subdued and quiet, conducted in the back parlor of one of his friends, John Orth. When the newly married couple arrived back at the City Brewery, though, they were greeted by the German brass band, and the party kicked into high gear. A letter written a few days later captures the evening's raucous mood: "Beer & wine commenced flowing like water." The account of Schutz's wedding goes on to somewhat fantastically indicate that this was literally the case, that beer seemed to literally be flowing throughout the brewery: "The high water mark reaching a point higher than the window sill, where a large amount of liquids escaped."

Likewise, Schutz's second marriage seemed to modulate between civil and riotous. When Johanna gave birth to his fourth child, Gustof, Schutz was sixty-three years old. Subsequently, she gave birth to his fifth and sixth children. Schutz had a reputation for his good humor, and some young patrons, as a goof, placed his name on the ballot to be county coroner, a position he won. As a further prank, one evening they hung a suit, boots and hat stuffed with straw from a downtown window. Schutz ordered what he believed was a corpse to be moved for an inquiry, and with a crowd gathered, the young men revealed the prank. When Schutz recognized he

At age sixty, Veit Schutz married his second wife, Hannah Lipke, in 1883. *SOHS #13028*.

had been fooled, he reportedly laughed and—in a thick German accent that a newspaper reporter tries to parrot—said, "Well, poys, coom up to te prewery und I'l gif efery von some peer." ("Well, boys, come up to the brewery and I'll give everyone some beer.")

Yet the mood at City Brewery was volatile. The *Democratic Times* reports that the "little man" slammed another man against kegs of beer and then had a chair smashed over his head in a fight over a billiard game. (The writer goes to lengths to list Schutz's height as only four foot, six inches, and marvels that he attacked a man much taller.) And there is an account in the *Sentinel* that Schutz was robbed at the City Brewery; he denied the incident, perhaps wanting to protect a reputation as a tough guy. There is another report, just shy from his two-year anniversary with Johanna, about a barroom fight, with "Mrs. Schutz" throwing glasses and bottles, and three men, including Schutz, taking cover under pool tables and behind the bar. Johanna was fined $5.00, plus $16.75 for medical bills for a "J.N. Jones," who had a swollen head.

And a year after that, Schutz was fined for selling beer without a license and received another fine a year after that for selling to minors. In 1890, a police blotter reports that a "respectable young man" was hit with a mallet at the City Brewery and temporarily lost his eyesight. There is another newspaper report about a man on Christmas Eve who, "under the soporific influence of Jacksonville lager," passed out at the brewery and had his gold watch and chain stolen.

But City Brewery was also host to some of Jacksonville's most popular social events. One of the final events was hosted by Johanna on February 12, 1892, to celebrate President Washington's birthday, who had been dead for nearly a century but maintained his aura of a national hero. (In 1885, Congress declared Washington's birthday a national holiday.) The two-dollar ticket included a hot meal.

Less than four months later, on June 3, 1892, Veit Schutz died. He was eulogized by Peter Britt, who called him a "good natured, jovial, whole soul man." With muted honesty appropriate for a funeral, Britt also indicated that Schutz was not perfect: "He may have had his faults," admitted Britt, "who have none?" Britt quickly added, "His merits many."

Yet, as gracious and fond as Britt might have been in his memories for Schutz, those sentiments apparently didn't extend to financial matters—or perhaps those emotions simply don't extend to Schutz's second wife, Johanna. At his death, Schutz still owed $1,400 from the mortgage he took out from Britt eighteen years earlier. In a sheriff's auction, Britt took over the brewery, as well as the cellars and caves, which he used for wine storage for the next two decades.

At the time of Schutz's death, City Brewery was the largest brewery in Southern Oregon. But when the Oregon & California Railroad completed a stretch of railroad from Portland to Ashland in 1884, the railway bypassed the county seat of Jacksonville in favor of a straight shot from Grants Pass to Ashland. Soon after, commerce and wealth began to drift steadily away from Jacksonville to the new boomtowns, where rival breweries began to spring up in Ashland, Medford and Grants Pass. At the time of Schutz's death, there were 8 licensed breweries in Southern Oregon, 32 in the entire state of Oregon and 2,011 nationwide—a number that wouldn't be matched for another hundred years.

2
1884–1908

Railroads and Pioneer Women

By the early 1880s, Adolphus Busch, the owner of a successful St. Louis–based brewery, had pioneered double-walled railcars, a relatively simple idea that insulated the boxcars to act like giant picnic coolers. Busch was the twenty-first of twenty-two children, born into a wealthy family who ran a brewery supply company in Germany. In 1857, at the age of eighteen, he immigrated to America. At first, though, he didn't take to the brewery business, even though St. Louis was an epicenter for German breweries, a perfect location, supplied with water from the Mississippi River and rife with caves to keep lagers cool.

Instead, three years after arriving in America, like many German Americans, he fought for the Union army in the Civil War. It wasn't until he returned from the battlefields that Busch began to edge into the beer business, first partnering with his new father-in-law, Eberhard Anheuser; together, they bought their first brewery. The pairing would have an enduring impact on the beer business worldwide as Anheuser-Busch.

A decade after purchasing their first brewery and with a desire to expand beyond the Midwest, Busch brainstormed the idea to leapfrog from railroad-side icehouse to icehouse and ship his products from coast to coast. In the process, their flagship lager Budweiser became the first beer available nationwide.

However, the railway had not yet reached the vast majority of Southern Oregon, which still remained mostly isolated from the rest of America—and some might say, insulated from expanding American empires like Budweiser.

A Pioneering History

Such isolation allowed breweries like Schutz's City Brewery and Wetterer's Eagle Brewery in Jacksonville to remain big fish in small towns.

But railroads were coming, drawing together American cities and towns like a grand connect-the-dots puzzle.

In 1862, President Abraham Lincoln signed into law the Pacific Railway Act to provide funding for a transcontinental railroad. Just as John F. Kennedy would one hundred years later when he declared that America would send rockets to the moon, Lincoln was reaching out to places like Jacksonville and Southern Oregon, which in the mid-nineteenth century were as remote to the rest of America as the moon. To reach Oregon had been a year-long trek from St. Louis for Meriwether Lewis and William Clark; even six or seven decades later, it was still a several-months-long plodding walk across the prairies and western mountain ranges. But, by the end of the nineteenth century, the great expanse of railroads would dramatically shorten that distance to a single week, and all done in the relative comfort of a chair.

But in the 1870s and early 1880s, Southern Oregon still was unconnected and remote. Travel between San Francisco and Portland remained a jarring thirteen-day stagecoach ride, primarily slowed by the tough mountain passes that lie like a giant's ribcage from Ashland to Roseburg. Even so, with determination and optimism in 1868, the California & Oregon Railroad drove the first spike in Portland for what the railroad men believed would be a 1,000-mile "express" line connecting Portland to San Francisco and essentially tying together two of the largest migrations yet in American history—the Oregon Trail and the California gold rush. By 1872, the rail had reached 180 miles south from Portland to Roseburg, a cowpoke town sitting at the rough edge between the Willamette Valley and the southern mountain ranges, and where a successful brewery had been set up by a German immigrant, Gottlieb Mehl, in 1861, a year before Lincoln declared the intent to tie together the country with rail lines. Like water to a fallow garden, the arrival of the railroad gave the brewery a jolt of extra life, with new commerce and settlers coming and going, and the so-called Rast Brewery in Roseburg lasted nearly until the twentieth century, when its namesake died in an accident.

For the next decade, the railroad failed to move an inch farther south from Roseburg. A stock market crash left the California & Oregon Railroad cash-poor—a consideration especially keen because, in Roseburg, the railroad had hit what would be the hardest stretch to lay track, requiring tunneling through mountainsides and building elaborate trusses alongside canyons. Even then, pitches remained so steep they required two engines to pull a train up.

Moreover, when the railroad did finally roll through Southern Oregon, it notably bypassed Jacksonville, the largest town in the region at the time, and the seat for Jackson County. The reasons it bypassed Jacksonville are somewhat murky. Technically, Jacksonville does not sit precisely on a plumb-straight line between Grants Pass and Ashland, but it is pretty darn close—and Jacksonville was a far more established and commercially important center than any other spot in Southern Oregon at that point. One rationale for bypassing Jacksonville, as engineers at the time pointed out, is that the city sits at a higher elevation from the more direct route out of Grants Pass and into Ashland; but even so, the pitch to climb into Jacksonville certainly was less challenging than other stretches in Southern Oregon. Another story is that the city refused to pony up $25,000 for the extra expense to slightly bow the rail line from its direct route and into Jacksonville.

Whatever the reason, it is clear that the lead engineer for the railroad project, David Loring, wasn't terribly concerned with hometown pride—or, at least not with Oregon home-grown pride—and instead of linking the railroad to the existing Jacksonville, he drew a straight line from Grants Pass to Ashland and directly five miles east from Jacksonville. There, he plotted a new town, a forty-block city that Loring named Medford, honoring his own hometown in Massachusetts. Instantly, Medford became the town for the future of Southern Oregon, and Jacksonville—and its two breweries—began a slow slide into history.

Like a magnet, the railroad drew men to the new city of Medford and to the newly energized towns of Ashland in the south and Grants Pass in the north. Perhaps inspired by the success of the two breweries in Jacksonville—then still the largest, most influential and certainly most civilized town in Southern Oregon—other prospectors tried to replicate the success of Wetterer's Eagle Brewery and Schutz's City Brewery. In 1884, the year the California & Oregon reached Ashland, two breweries sprang up overnight: the Ashland Brewery and the Charles Wurz Brewery. Both were short-lived, though, and vanish from records a year later. Another brewery opens in Ashland in 1885, Reifel and Company, and also lasts for one year. Likewise, in 1884 in Medford—the town that would quickly eclipse Jacksonville in population and civic importance and eventually steal the county seat designated—the Paul Breistenstein Brewery opened. It closed in 1886.

In spite of the flash-in-the-pan breweries, there were other, more meticulous and cautious men—or, at least, men a little more studied and less quick to the trigger—who went about the business of opening breweries in Southern Oregon.

A Pioneering History

Not surprisingly, many of these men came from Jacksonville. In the mix is William Heeley, who, in 1883, the year before the railroad arrived in Southern Oregon, married Joseph Wetterer's widow, Fredericka. Records list Heely as an "employee" at the Eagle Brewery, and some even hint that he was a brewer there, but there is nothing in his background to support this idea. Decades later, Fredericka's granddaughter recollected in detail how her grandfather Joseph Wetterer ran the brewery and fondly remembered her grandmother governing over the company's finances and operations. She breezily dismissed the idea that Heeley had anything to do with the brewery, besides hanging around it.

In reality, Heeley was a roustabout, a habitual prospector, who even at the age of seventy-five rushed off to the gold fields in Alaska.

Born in 1826 in Yorkshire, England, he was drawn to America by the California gold rush, but he did not arrive in America until 1851, and even then, late to the party, he stalled for two years on the East Coast before crossing the continent. By the time he arrived on the West Coast, most of the gold prospectors had already dispersed from central California to spots like Jacksonville. Heeley seems to have had minor luck with mining in Southern Oregon, and he purchased a ranch.

But his fortunes must have been modest, because he spent the next couple decades working as a hired hand and trying "mule packing," although the value of delivering goods from the California coast had diminished since the days when Schutz first ran those routes, as the passes had become far more traveled and far less dangerous.

In 1883, Heeley sold his ranch, married Fredericka (three years a widow) and moved into the home adjacent to the Eagle Brewery, along with her five surviving children.

But Heeley didn't settle down. A year later, a police report records that he beat up the brewer at the Eagle Brewery. Decades later, at the dawn of the new century and the age of seventy-five, Heeley split from his home with Fredericka in Jacksonville to prospect for gold in Alaska. But by the time he arrived, the gold rush was a few years after its peak—and he soon returned to Jacksonville. He died in 1906 at the age of eighty.

But in the 1880s, newly married to Fredericka and with fresh opportunities in Medford and Grants Pass, Heeley seemed to consider breweries his new frontier. In 1884, the Eagle Brewery changed its name to the William and Fredericka Heeley Brewery, and the following summer, he was in Medford scouting for properties to open a brewery. According to the *Democratic Times*, he had teamed up with a friend from Jacksonville, and together they leased a building and planned to open the Brewery Saloon. But nothing seems to have materialized with that plan—and in fact, there wasn't to be a lasting brewery in Medford until 1892.

By the following summer, Heeley had moved on to Grants Pass and reportedly partnered with yet another man from Jacksonville, Fred Grob, who ran a baked goods store and saloon in Jacksonville that sold beer, rye bread, Limburger cheese and, exotically, oysters. A German immigrant, Grob also was a member of the Red Man Lodge with Schutz.

In May 1886, the *Oregon Sentinel* gleeful announced the partner had plotted a location, adjacent to Gilbert Creek, a narrow waterway that traced along the northern edge of the business district. The article points out that they were digging a well for "artesian water" to supply the brewery. In a tone expressing either hometown bravado or an intentional slight to out-of-town brewing operations, the brief article concludes: "It is to be hoped the proprietors of this institution will manufacture a better quality of malt liquors than the rest of the brewers in Oregon."

But by the following year, when the Grants Pass Brewery officially opened, Heeley had vanished from any role in the enterprise, as had Grob, who returned to Jacksonville to run his cheese and oysters store. The new proprietor was listed as William Neurath, and he boldly hired a brewer from San Francisco to run the Grants Pass Brewery. More than a century later, the building once again ushered in a new era of breweries in Southern Oregon and became home to Climate City Brewery (see chapter 7).

During this time, as new breweries were taking root in Grants Pass, and soon Medford, the breweries in Jacksonville were still largely business as usual—that is, with the glaring exception that Fredericka Heeley (formerly Wetterer) had taken charge of the Eagle Brewery after her first husband's death. By this time, she was an old hand at managing breweries.

In 2018, the Oregon Historical Society curated a *200 Years of Oregon Beer* exhibit and, as part of the display, included a placard declaring Fredericka Wetterer as the first woman brewer in Oregon; however, that claim may be overreaching slightly. It is not clear that she was actually brewing. Instead, there are notes and newspaper articles about other brewers at the Eagle Brewery, hinting that she was not actually making the beer but hired brewers.

Even if Fredericka was not stirring the pots, though, she clearly was managing the brewery. The Southern Oregon Historical Society in Medford has folders full of meticulous notes and receipts from these years. There is a handwritten receipt from H. Weinhard on January 20, 1880, catching up on some past-due amounts, paid in U.S. gold coin and with a balance of $66.83. In September

1880, she purchased a saccharometer (used to measure sugar content) for $2.50 from Scherr, Bach & Lux, a hops and brewer material store in San Francisco. There is a receipt in shaky handwriting for "one bale of hops" from a Eugene shop, but no price indicated, and another for a bale of hops from Roseburg, for $225, including the hauling and delivery to Jacksonville. In 1880, she bought $75 worth of Havana cigars. Interestingly, she also maintained a subscription to Chicago-based the *Western Brewer*, an indication that she was connected to the wider world of brewing. (Along with publications like the *Western Brewer*, the network of brewers was increasingly connected throughout America. In 1862, a group of New York–based brewers formed the United States Brewers' Association. Like Wetterer, the founder was from Baden, Germany, and the organization comprised almost exclusively German Americans, so much so that German was the group's official language. There is no indication that Fredericka was a member, though.)

Fredericka Wetterer, unknown date. *SOHS #21077*.

Interestingly, after her first husband's death, Fredericka seems to have gone through a transformation of confidence—or perhaps she just ended her mourning period and came into her own. In the year after his death, Fredericka signed receipts with the header of Joseph Wetterer with no indication that business had changed. But by 1880, a year after his death, she had begun crossing off his name and writing in her own and replacing "proprietor" on contracts with the feminized "proprietrix."

More broadly, although brewing and owning breweries largely has been a male-dominated industry throughout American history—and certainly continues to be nearly exclusively so into the twenty-first century—for a few decades in the late nineteenth century, Southern Oregon was an exception to that rule. During those years, Fredericka was not the only woman running a brewery in Southern Oregon—nearly half of the operational breweries in the region were run by women at that time.

In 1875, Mary Mehl moved to Coquille with her husband, Gottlieb Mehl, a German brewer seventeen years her senior who had arrived in Oregon

Receipt for Eagle Brewery—note Fredericka has crossed off her husband's name. *Oregon State University archives.*

in 1849 and since changed his first name to John. The Johnny Appleseed of nineteenth-century Oregon brewers, Mehl established the Rast Brewery in Roseburg in 1861, leaving ten years later when the original brewery burned down after a fire started in the malt house. (Although, according to the 2009 *Distilled in Oregon*, he retained some stake in the enterprise, as his wife eventually sold the interest in 1898, but that report is disputed by other records.) Mehl seems to have chased opportunities. In 1872, he set up another brewery, about twenty-five miles north along the railroad line in Oakland, Oregon. Four years later, he relocated one more time to Coquille near the Oregon coast, where timber was fueling a booming economy. For each new venture, Mehl traveled with his wife—and she was clearly knowledgeable about the brewery business. Born in 1840 in Tennessee, Mary seems to have met Mehl when her family moved to Oregon, presumably in the late 1850s or early 1860s.

Like the Schutz brewery in Jacksonville, the Mehls called their operation in Coquille the City Brewery. They began selling ten- and fifteen-gallon kegs directly to saloons and logging camps and, not surprising, quickly became popular. But, like the brewery in Roseburg, in 1889, a fire consumed the City Brewery in Coquille. This time, the Mehls stuck around, and the loggers helped them rebuild. In return, the Mehls began a tradition: giving away free beer to firefighters returning after a fire. Successful and well-liked, by 1892, the Mehls planned to expand to the nearby coastal and port town of Bandon. But, before they could open the brewery, John Mehl died (coincidentally, the same year that Schutz died in Jacksonville).

Mary Mehl inherited the brewery and thereafter proved to possess a full pint of business acumen, enough not only to continue to operate the Coquille brewery but also to expand into the new brewery. She quickly changed the name of the City Brewery in Coquille to the Mary Mehl Brewery and, a year later, opened another Mary Mehl Brewery in Bandon, Oregon.

Farther inland, in Grants Pass, was perhaps the most colorful and flamboyant of the three women to own breweries in Southern Oregon in the late nineteenth century. In 1890, fifty-five-year-old Fredericka closed the Eagle Brewery, though she lived another twenty-six years, until 1916. And in 1895, Mary Mehl sold her brewery in Bandon to a brewer from nearby Randolph, Oregon, another gold rush town several miles up the Coquille River from the coast (and now a ghost town). But in Grants Pass, Marie Kienlen, a woman who was both from a different culture and from a more modern era than the other two women, continued to operate her brewery until Prohibition shut her down in the early twentieth century—and she did not go quietly.

While Mary Mehl and Fredericka Wetterer-Heeley were hardworking pioneer women, Marie was a flamboyant Frenchwoman. Married—or perhaps just living as a common-law spouse—Marie had come to Grants Pass after absconding from St. Paul, Minnesota, with Eugene Kienlen, a German man who had immigrated at age fifteen in 1865. He had lived in Minnesota for nineteen years before meeting a French immigrant three or six years younger, or perhaps a decade older, depending on the source of information.

Marie and Eugene had ditched the Midwest (and Eugene's wife and children) and arrived in Southern Oregon in 1886, where Eugene took up farming for a few years before purchasing the brewery in Grants Pass from William Neurath in 1891. (In other accounts, it seems as if Eugene and Marie started to tell a different story, as historical records began to list Eugene and Marie as natives from Alsace-Lorraine, France, implying that they immigrated to America together.)

It is remarkable to note the differences between the three women—or, more specifically, to consider that both Fredericka Wetterer and Mary Mehl both arrived in Oregon after traveling months in ox-drawn carts. In particular, Fredericka had a harrowing trek, arriving in America after a fifty-day voyage across the Atlantic Ocean at the age of fifteen and then spent two years living in St. Louis before a five-month trek to Oregon City.

In an interview, Fredericka's granddaughter told a story about Fredericka being kidnapped by Native Americans along the way (and then presumably ransomed back).

Marie was only thirty years younger than Fredericka and twenty younger than Mary, but by the time she moved across the continent to Oregon in 1886, the journey has been shortened from months to a few days—and all in the relative smooth ease of a railcar.

Eugene and Marie Kienlen were seemingly well-to-do, if not a touch eccentric. (Marie was known to walk around Grants Pass with her two parrots perched on her shoulders.) They purchased the brewery operations in 1891 and, in 1899, purchased the property as well.

They also purchased other tracts of land, including a city block along G Street after a fire lay waste to the buildings there. In 1900, Eugene rebuilt the section of town, including a stylish and ornate two-story brick building with a baroque-style tower rising above the second floor. An article in the *Rogue River Courier* at the time calls it "a very handsome edifice [that]...gives a very metropolitan appearance to that portion of the city." With some editorial license hinting at the growing anti-drinking sentiment in Grants Pass, the article adds, "The building is far more creditable than the use to which it will be put, as it will be occupied as a saloon, another corner saloon."

Indeed, the building served as a saloon and hostel for goldminers until local prohibition in 1908 before transforming into a butcher shop. In 1982, the building was added to the National Register of Historic Places.

The 1900 census lists the couple living at 388 Fifth Street, just two blocks from the brewery, and now the site of a Napa Auto Parts store. (The census has plenty of mistakes or, at least, conflicting information, such as listing her name as Mary T. and placing her birthdate as 1845, which could be true and would make her Eugene's senior by a decade and recast their narrative. Her middle name is "Theresa," and it is possible that the census taker simply mis-wrote the information. Her gravestone lists her birth year as 1856, and other sources give 1859.) Neighbors in the census are listed as

Perhaps the first woman brewer in Oregon, Marie Kienlen, with parrots. Josephine County Historical Society.

"groceryman," "brick-maker," "gold miner" and "druggist." The Kienlens had two servants living with them at the premises; notably, theirs is the only family on the block with live-in servants.

The reports about the Grants Pass Brewery are rambunctious. The Kienlens employed five men, and it was a beehive of activity. Even years later, grown men recalled in newspaper articles about frequenting the brewery as young boys and fetching buckets of beer for a quarter to deliver to workers or parents in the area—or sometimes to drink themselves.

"The heavy-set woman was known for her parrots, which would often sit on her shoulder outside in her garden on the east side of the property," reports the *Daily Courier* in a 2003 article. The article goes on to quote a then-ninety-three-year-old man, Bill Young of Grants Pass, who, according to the article, "used to walk from Jordan Street near the old Roosevelt School and pick up a 25-cent pail of beer for his father." Young was in his preteen years when the Grants Brewery was in operation and recalled, "We'd cuss the parrot and she'd run us off. We learned him some bad language."

What is particularly interesting is that there is evidence that Marie truly was a brewer. At some point, she earned a diploma from the New York Brewers Association, and her obituary specifically listed her career as a brewer for five years, which, if true, Marie—and not Fredericka—is arguably the first woman brewer in Oregon.

But the new century was not kind to Marie. In 1902, another fire ripped through the northern edge of Grants Pass's business district, and the brewery was hit hardest of several buildings, suffering $12,000 in damages (or $350,000 in contemporary value). "The losses are heavy, but insured," says the *Rogue River Courier*. They rebuilt quickly, this time with a sturdy brick building that still stands today. In 2014, it again housed a brewery, the Climate City Brewery (see chapter 7).

In 1904, Eugene died. He had been sick for three years and transferred all of his property and wealth to Marie. Even so, she was ordered by the court to compensate $7,000 to Eugene's wife and children from Minnesota.

And, in 1908, more than a decade before the rest of the country went "dry," a local ordinance for prohibition shut down the brewery production in Grants Pass.

The twentieth century did not start well for Marie.

3
1908-1934

End of an Era: Prohibition!

Much is attributed to Prohibition for ending a golden era for American breweries, but in Southern Oregon, that simply isn't true—or, at least not entirely correct.

Already, by the early twentieth century, local breweries throughout America were dwindling in numbers. With an all-time high of 4,131 breweries nationwide in 1873, new market pressures soon and rapidly pushed that number down. At the time, beer production had risen from one to nine million barrels over two decades, and consumption rates were pacing that growth. Per capita rates had risen and would continue to rise to fifteen gallons by the end of the century, a 240 percent inflation over four decades—not to mention during an era when America's population doubled, essentially creating a near 500 percent increase in beer drinking since the first wave of German brewers had washed up on America's shores in 1848.

But improved production efficiency coupled with easier distribution (not to mention the invention of the crown bottle cap) eliminated a vital premise: That local breweries were necessary to provide beer. Between 1880 and 1910, the number of independent breweries in America more than halved to 1,500. And with the consolidation of the beer industry, the locally grown brewery became a quaint idea for the past century—and established a trend that would pick up again right after Prohibition ended in 1933.

Finally linked to the rest of the state by 1884—and, by extension, to the rest of the country—much of Southern Oregon was not immune to those same

A Pioneering History

History of Active Breweries in the United States
Total Number of Active Breweries (BA) Since 1873

- 1873: HISTORICAL PEAK OF 4,131 BREWERIES
- 1920–1933: PROHIBITION
- 1978: H.R. 1337 SIGNED BY JIMMY CARTER LEGALIZES HOMEBREWING
- 1995: BOSTON BEER CO. IPO (SAM ADAMS)
- 2005: THE LAST ANNUAL DROP IN ACTIVE BREWERIES WAS A DECADE AGO
- 2015: THE 1873 PEAK HAS BEEN SURPASSED!

BREWERS ASSOCIATION HISTORICAL "ACTIVE BREWERIES"

SOURCE: Brewers Association. *NOTE: 2016 Active count as of Nov 30, 2016

VINEPAIR — VINEPAIR.COM

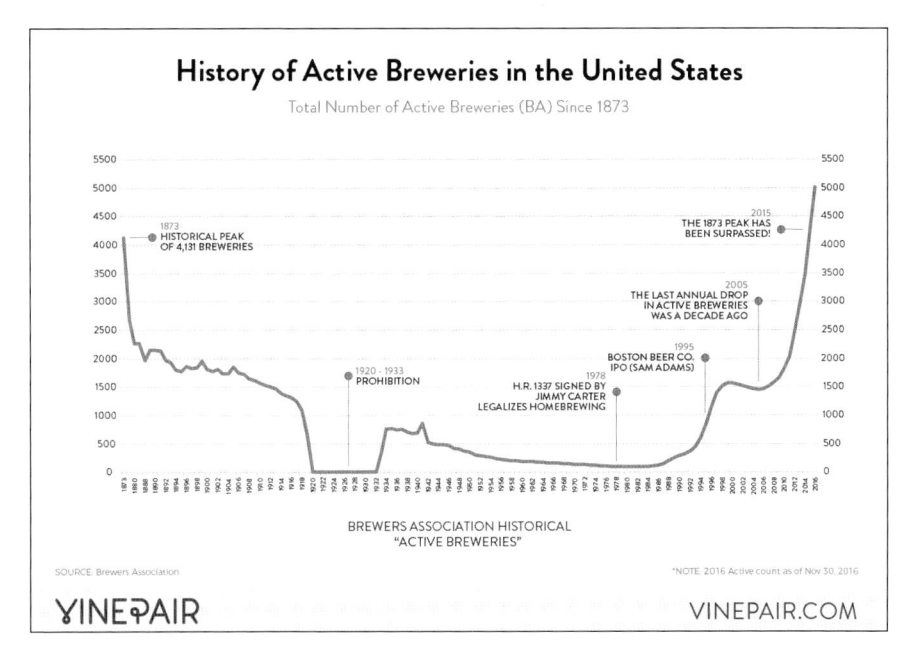

The number of breweries in America first peaked in 1873, a number not reached again until 2015. *Courtesy of VinePair/Vinepair.com.*

market pressures. By 1900, the first generation of brewers in Southern Oregon was gone. Gottlieb "John" Mehl died in 1892, and his wife sold their breweries a few years later. Fredericka Wetterer carried on the Eagle Brewery for eleven years after her husband died but closed shop in 1890 as commerce drifted away from Jacksonville to the railroad corridor along the path connecting Grants Pass, Medford and Ashland. In 1892, when Veit Schutz died, the largest brewery in Southern Oregon ceased operations—facilities that, innovative in their day, were already outdated.

Schutz's City Brewery was eventually taken over by his friend Peter Britt, who used the cellars and storage to expand his wine production and distribution—and set an enduring trend in Southern Oregon, one that splits the regional beverage industry between beer and wine producers. Along with honey, pears, peaches and apples, Britt was producing about one thousand gallons of wine each year and shipping them as far away as Wyoming.

But when Britt died in 1905, the building, storage cellars and caves were abandoned, except for a brief moment in 1907 when the space served as a classroom after the town's primary school burned down. Four years after that, a local newspaper reports that E.P. Bowers, an old prospector "well known in this vicinity," was ill at the old brewery building, where he had been making his home—between the lines, this seems to hint that E.P. Bower was a vagrant and the brewery had become a flophouse.

Decades later, Jacksonville fell on its own hard times, largely bypassed by history and its glory days faded. The old brewery was sagging under its own weight and neglect. In 1958, worried that the building would collapse onto the rural highway that now bordered the property, city officials took bids for its removal. All that remains today are some of the collapsed, rock-lined caves.

Even so, the number of breweries in Southern Oregon held steady into the twentieth century, as a new generation of brewers replaced pioneers Schutz and Wetterer, especially in the towns removed from the railroad corridor, like in Klamath Falls to the east and Coos Bay to the west.

Moreover, the new breweries popping up in Southern Oregon at the turn of the century were doing so with more modern equipment and pushing production capacity from 300 to 1,500 barrels each year.

But even so, their stories are simple tales of arriving at the party too late.

Perhaps the greatest potential for success was a massive four-story, entire-city-block warehouse in North Bend, a port town adjacent to Coos Bay (then known as Marshfield). Although the area was isolated from the interior of Oregon, it is a bustling sea hub, as quick a trip to San Francisco by water as it was overland to Jacksonville. Notably, Coos Bay/Marshfield/North Bend served as a shipping center for raw lumber as well as a number of shops milling Oregon's wood into tables and fancy doors. The brewery was the second in the area, joining the Marshfield Brewery. Opened by Charlie

By the 1950s, Veit Schutz's City Brewery had fallen into disrepair and was slated for demolition. *Oregon Hops & Beer Archives.*

A Pioneering History

Thorn, the new brewery was a large and ambitious enterprise, and in 1907, a year before Coos Bay County considered prohibition, the brewery opened with a steady production of kegs and bottles and a far-reaching marketing scheme for its "Pacific Pride" beer.

More common at the turn of the century, though, was that the existing and new breweries were snapped up by big-city investors or other breweries who recognized that these new facilities offered opportunities to expand their own production.

In 1898, John Rast, who had operated a brewery in Roseburg since 1861, died in an accident. That same year, another brewery opened in town, the Roseburg Brewing and Ice Co., a modern operation that covered an entire city block and not only produced beer, but also ice, which had become a valuable commodity, picked up by the railroad companies and used for keeping railcars refrigerated. Started by Max Weiss, a German immigrant and the son of a brewer, the new facility in Roseburg housed a bottling machine that could produce a whirling two hundred bottles per hour and fifteen to fifty kegs of beer daily. It was a massive jump in production rates. But perhaps reading the writing on the wall, in 1905—just six years after opening—Weiss sold his operation to investors from Portland for $50,000. In 1908, the county went dry, and in turn, the investors retrofitted the facilities and contracted with Southern Pacific railroad to have a supply of one thousand tons of block ice ready at all times.

Likewise, in Medford a brewery opened in 1893, the Southern Oregon Beer, Ice and Cold Storage (a name that would be picked up again more than a century later and be more familiarly known as S.O.B.). Directly across from the railroad, the brewery occupied a prime location, and owner G.W. Bashford spared no expense. In spite of the big plans and a great location for receiving its ingredients—like barley from eastern Oregon and hops from the Willamette Valley—the brewery lacked vital access to good water. An article in the *Democratic Times* reports that the brewery was digging a well at the site and hoped to find "artesian water."

Already, it had reached a 350-foot depth with no results. (For a point of comparison, the brewery in Grants Pass, which specifically chose its location for the source of water, only needed to dig a well 30 feet deep.) A month later, the *Democratic Times* reports that the owners were still digging and that the brewery's engineer "had the middle finger of his right hand so badly mangled by the machinery that it was found necessary to amputate it."

All told, the Southern Oregon Brewery, as it was more commonly called—or, alternatively, Medford Brewing Company—was a slow-moving train wreck: By the time construction began again, the *Democratic Times* was still banging the drum for the brewery and announced that "the Medford brewery will be ready for business before warm weather comes, which will be glad tidings to the bibulously inclined."

The plans for the Southern Oregon Brewery were as ambitious as any in the region for that date. Notably, the owners took into account proximity to the railway and coupled the brewery with an ice production plant. As much as beer was part of the business plan, the production of ice was critical for additional revenue. A report in the state business registry notes, "The Southern Oregon Brewing, Ice and Cold Storage Company building has a frontage of thirty-two feet, the depth being eighty-six feet, and the height being thirty-eight feet. It is operated by steam of fifty horsepower, and has a daily capacity of five tons of ice and six tons of cold storage."

It seemed as if G.W. Bashford was sparing no expense. In addition to the ice production, the facilities produced fifteen barrels of beer every day, and the brewery included a malt house, two stories high. In April 1893, G.W. Bashford traveled to San Francisco to hire a brewer, and a week later, the newspaper announced the new brewer's arrival: "Gotlieb Hess, an expert brewer direct from Germany, arrived in Medford yesterday morning. He will have charge of the Medford brewery, and while his services come high they are quite necessary."

But, as spring melted into summer the brewery still wasn't open. Another friendly article reports: "Frank Pfluger, of Portland, is at work putting in the new vats and tubs for the Southern Oregon Brewing Co. It begins to look like there was a positive assurance that this institution will be in readiness to commence operations now pretty soon—and when they do they can give the laugh to those who predicted such a thing would never be." The final jab seemed to indicate that the delays in opening the facility had amassed a certain number of doubters.

By the heat of summer, the facilities finally opened—at least the ice production side of operations. A July article in the *Democratic Times* gleefully announces: "The new ice wagon of the Southern Oregon Brewing Company appeared on the streets of Medford yesterday, making the rounds of ice delivery. It is most decidedly a beauty and an 'up to date' metropolitan turnout. The lettering on the sides is the work of Sherman, the painter, and it's a good job. The word 'Ice' gives one the chills to look at it—it's weighted down with imitation ice."

It seems as if Southern Oregon Brewing lurched into business in the nick of time. Less than two weeks later, some of the investors lost faith in

G.W. Bashford and filed a lawsuit against him. "A little trouble, or more proper, a misunderstanding, exists among the directors and stockholders of the Southern Oregon Brewing, Ice and Cold Storage Company," reports the ever-sympathetic *Democratic Times*, "and in consequence of which I.L. Hamilton has been appointed receiver. From one of the stockholders we learn that by the appointment of a receiver it does not necessarily follow that the company is insolvent." Already, building the facility had cost $25,000 (about $650,000 in current value), while only earning "about seven hundred" ($18,000), according to the article.

Trouble continued to nip at Bashford's heels. In late August, the new brewer—"Gotlieb Hess, an expert brewer direct from Germany"—was arrested. Again, the *Democratic Times* provides an update: "Mr. Hess, who has been acting as brewer for the Medford Brewing Co., was arrested this week, charged with an assault with a dangerous weapon. Justice Dunlap was called upon to adjust the difficulty and held the defendant to answer, placing his bonds at $250, which were furnished."

A day later, Hess had been replaced by a brewer from Portland. The *Democratic Times* flatly reports: "Herman Lenhart, of Portland, is the new brewer at the Medford Brewing Company's establishment."

By December, Southern Oregon Brewing finally released its first batch of beer. By now, though, the tone in the *Democratic Times* had calmed down from its original cheerleading, and the review is modest: "The Medford Brewery has placed its beer on sale…and those who have sampled it say it is just as good as the average and in some respects several notches ahead."

In December, G.W. Bashford also outright purchased the brewery and ice facilities from investors. Once in operation, the brewery made a big leap forward for production, producing a reported 1,500 barrels each year, an amount five times what Schutz's brewery was churning out just a decade earlier.

The brewery, though, seemed as much about beer as producing ice for the railway stop across the street, and in February 1897, the *Daily Capital Journal* in Salem reports that "the Medford brewery and ice works was purchased today by E. Merz, of Portland." The small business report also notes the facility "contains the latest improved machinery, and is valued at $15,000"—a poor investment for G.W. Bashford who, only three years earlier, reportedly had invested as much as $25,000.

Three weeks later, the facility was officially renamed the Medford Brewing Company, even though the new owners—including some of the best-known brewery owners in the Pacific Northwest—were based in Portland, not

Southern Oregon. On March 3, 1897, the *Daily Capital Journal* followed up on its previous report, explaining, "The Medford Brewing Company incorporated today. The principal place of business is given as Medford, but the well-known signatures of Henry Weinhard, Paul Wessinger and Elias Merz are affixed to the articles, indicating that it is merely a branch of a Portland house."

The facilities were overhauled to serve as a warehouse for Weinhard's Portland-produced beers and for selling ice, and, by 1902, it had dropped the façade and began to advertise under Weinhard's brand.

(An interesting side note to the fiasco with the Southern Oregon Brewing, Ice and Storage/Medford Brewing Company is that, after his assault charges in 1893, the former brewer, Gotlieb Hess, "an expert brewer direct from Germany," bounced from Medford to Jacksonville, where he had his own plans to reboot one of the breweries there; first, the Eagle Brewery, closed by Fredericka three years earlier. When that didn't happen, he went for the City Brewery, empty after Veit Schutz died a year prior. According to the "Local Notes" in the *Democratic Times*: "Gottlieb Hess, a first-class brewer, has leased the old Wetterer brewery and will put it in shape for business." The article adds, "He was for a time in the employ of the S.O. Brewing Co. of Medford." With no reference to the previous lease of the Eagle Brewery [the "old Wetterer brewery"], in December 1893, the *Democratic Times* reports: "Gottlieb Hess and A. Lutkemeier, who have had much experience in the business, have leased the Veit Schutz brewery and will take possession on the 1st of January. The former has already established a reputation as a brewer, and will doubtless manufacture a first-class quality of beer." Again, there is no movement on these plans—and, eventually, Peter Britt took over the building and its cellars himself for wine production and storage.)

In addition to the larger market pressures and trends of consolidations, local prohibition loomed like an encroaching, humorless army on the horizon. Not a new idea, prohibition had been in the state's DNA since its inception when, in 1844, a provisional government set up in Oregon City banned the manufacture and sale of "ardent spirits" in the Oregon Territory. A year later, that law was rolled back, allowing the manufacture of liquor, but imposing heavy licensing fees and a $100 fine for selling to Native Americans.

Likewise, throughout America in the 1850s, other states set up beer and spirits limitations and outright bans. Starting with Maine in 1851, twelve additional states restricted or outright banned alcohol. These prohibitions were met with riots and, by 1861, at the outbreak of the Civil War, completely

A Pioneering History

Prohibition pins. *Oregon Historical Society.*

gone—in part, because beer and liquor offered a lucrative market for the newly created IRS to tap for revenue to fund the Union armies.

In 1887, a proposed ordinance in Oregon for prohibition failed miserably, crushed three to one. It was another seventeen years before Oregon considered banning beer and alcohol—and when Oregon did ban beer, wine and booze, it was not one swift motion but an uneven patchwork of county and local ordinances before a complete statewide ban.

By the close of the nineteenth century, once again, there was a groundswell for prohibition, in part because drinking habits had spiraled somewhat out of control, with most American men drinking thirty-six gallons of beer each year and seven gallons of whiskey, numbers twice as much as current consumption rates. Organizations like the Woman's Christian Temperance Union stumped and rallied around Oregon, and one by one, counties began to vote on prohibition.

Creating an uneven enforcement of liquor laws, a so-called home rule in Oregon allowed cities and towns to enact their own liquor prohibition laws, regardless of county regulations. For example, when Lane County in the Willamette Valley voted itself dry in 1910, the city of Eugene, home to the University of Oregon, adhered to the rule, but directly across the Willamette River, the lumber and working-class town of Springfield rejected prohibition and remained a "wet" city, reportedly with a steady stream of college students across the river.

In Southern Oregon, the towns and counties also were a patchwork of bans and allowances. Coos County and Klamath Falls held off prohibition, but both Josephine County and its county seat, Grants Pass, strongly favored prohibition. (In an apt parallel, one hundred years later, while the rest of Oregon allowed for the sale of marijuana, Grants Pass banned its sale.)

Especially in Grants Pass, opinions about beer and alcohol sales seemed particularly set along ethnic and class divisions. At the time, Grants Pass was struggling to shed its frontier days and emerge as a modern twentieth-century city—or, at least, one segment of the city was trying to do so. But the city remained peppered with Wild West elements. There were no paved roads in the city, and four-horse stagecoaches were the primary transportation to points east and west of the city, off the railroad corridor. Grants Pass also gained a reputation as a rowdy town. Two more breweries sprang up, including a production house run by a German immigrant named George Walter that was pushing out five barrels a day. There were twelve saloons for a population of roughly three thousand, although Marie Kienlen's Grants Pass Brewery remained ground zero, with young boys serving as "runners," fetching their pails of beer for twenty-five cents and dashing them to thirsty workers and roustabouts alike. By 1905, in an attempt to place a lid on the simmering pot, city council capped the number of liquor licenses at one per five hundred residents, meaning the city's population would need to nearly triple before it would issue any new liquor licenses.

In 1908, the Grants Pass City Council looked for even stronger measures, and a citywide prohibition was introduced. So strong were the feelings against drinking that the city council recognized it would need to postpone paving local roads if prohibition succeeded, as prohibition would eliminate a massive tax base—a cutting-off-their-noses-to-spite-their-faces sentiment.

The 1908 vote split largely along ethnic lines, with the southern, German sections of town voting against prohibition. Even so, the measure carried. (Interestingly, the southern districts proved a strong enough voting block to quash a proposed ordinance banning hogs in town.) Prohibition in Grants Pass was briefly rejected in 1911, but by 1912, it was back on the books—and stayed there for more than twenty years.

A Pioneering History

In November 1914, both Washington and Oregon adopted statewide bans. With women's suffrage approved in 1912, it was the first election in which women could vote—with three out of four women in Oregon voting in favor of prohibition, it was a critical swing vote. Oregon's Governor Oswald West signed an Executive Order for statewide prohibition, even though, curiously, the governor owned a hops farm.

Five years later, with three-quarter of the states in America ratifying the Eighteenth Amendment, Congress adopted federal Prohibition laws, and soon after passed the Volstead Act, which clamped down an outright ban on intoxicating beverages.

Reactions to national Prohibition by the brewery owners were varied. In Medford, the Weinhard company, perhaps with a mentality of keeping your enemies close, supplied ice for a temperance party in a city park. Its founder, Henry Weinhard, died in 1904, just as the first prohibition laws were being set in place in Oregon. In North Bend, Charlie Thorn shut down his new and massive four-story facility on the coast and poured the brewed beer into the streets. The Klamath Falls Brewery, which opened in 1878, simply closed its doors and walked away. For a brief moment in 1934, the facilities reopened when Prohibition was repealed, but almost as quickly it closed.

In Grants Pass, though, Marie Kienlen stubbornly tried to hold on. She was particularly targeted by the men on the city council and reportedly did not bend to their demands or admonishments. After Grants Pass went dry in 1908, the *Klamath Falls Evening Herald* reports that Marie was re-engineering her kettles and coolers for "manufacturing denatured alcohol," a product that had its legitimate industrial uses but also found more dangerous and shady uses by bootleggers. The article goes on to claim, "The Grants Pass brewery is the first of these institutions."

The very month after Prohibition closed the brewery's beer production, Marie married Sam Kienlen, a man alternatively noted in records as her brother-in-law or as her deceased husband's nephew. The business was renamed the Grants Pass Bottling Company and overhauled its kettles and coolers to produce soda pop. (It is unclear what happened to the idea for denatured alcohol.)

Like Weinhard in Portland, which survived Prohibition by producing root beer, vanilla cream, orange cream and black cherry sodas, Marie also legitimately produced soda pop at the facility during those years.

But it seems as if the soda pop production was, at least in part, a smoke screen. Marie did not move out any of the brewing equipment, and five years after Prohibition was first enacted in Grants Pass, there was a raid on the former brewery. Her new husband, Samael, was arrested and "two dray-loads of 'wet' goods are stored for evidence," according to the February 13, 1913 *Rogue River Courier*. Samuel was eventually fined $500 for illicit kegs. (In 1916, Samuel left Marie and Grants Pass permanently.)

During the 1920s, Marie seemed to go 100 percent legitimate, selling candy, soft drinks (still presumably manufactured on-site) and, according to one report, parrots. It is difficult to accurately track her financial fortunes during these Prohibition years. Shortly after Prohibition was enacted statewide, she purchased a large plot of land in the business district, which certainly suggests that she still had some funds, but as the 1920s closed out—and the Great Depression set in—it seemed as if her fortunes had dwindled. Although she still reportedly walked around town with parrots on her shoulders, there also were reports that her wealth had faded and she was living in one section of the brewery.

At the age seventy-five, she died in 1934, a year after Prohibition was lifted.

4
1880s–1950s

Hops Keep an Industry Afloat

Just as breweries in Oregon were shut down in the early twentieth century, remarkably, another beer-related industry boomed in the state: hops growing. The timing is ironic: During the very years that Prohibition blanketed the state of Oregon—first with county restrictions starting in 1908 and then, by 1916, as a statewide ban—Oregon began a fast and steady climb to the peak of hops production in the world. Said differently, during the very same years that beer was outlawed in America, Oregon became the number-one grower in the world for an essential ingredient for beer, providing aroma, spice, flavor and bitterness.

At first, hops production was simply enough to supply the breweries, and homebrewers, in Oregon, but then it quickly outpaced the beer industry in the state. In 1850, a couple years before the first breweries opened in Oregon, there were only 8 pounds of hops reportedly grown in the state. By 1860, the year after Oregon became a state and with a half-dozen breweries operating in the state at the time, there were 493 pounds of hops reportedly grown in Oregon—still a small amount, but enough to flavor the beers being produced in Oregon at the time.

While hops came into favor with the craft beer boom in the 1990s and beyond, the punch-in-the-mouth flavors of IPAs were not much in favor before then, and nineteenth- and mid-twentieth-century brewers were not delivering triple hopped or dry-hopped beers, or anything like the hop-crazed concoctions that are familiar now. For the beers like Undertow Imperial from Portal and Hopportunity Knocks from Caldera, typically two pounds of hops are required per barrel, if not more. For more restrained levels of hoppiness, though, a half pound for each barrel suffices, and the early lagers were faint in hops. With mid-nineteenth-century breweries producing approximately 150 to 300 barrels annually, one hundred pounds was probably enough for Veit Schutz or Fredericka Wetterer per year. In one receipt from 1879, Fredericka purchased one bale of hops—about two hundred pounds—from a broker in Roseburg. That purchase presumably held her production for the entire year. In a file at the Southern Oregon Historical Society, there is another receipt from a year later for a bale of hops from a Eugene-based broker for another bale; she paid twenty-eight dollars.

Over next half century, from the 1880s until the end of Prohibition in 1933, the minor industry of hops farming ballooned to a major agriculture crop in Oregon, a growth motivated as much by opportunities within the state and region, as by failures in other hops-growing parts of the country—and, in particular, Oregon growers began to export their crops beyond the breweries in the state.

For most of the nineteenth century, it was New England, and particularly New York, that ruled the hops market in America. The growers in New York lost their crown with a massive migration from the East Coast into the then frontier of the Midwest. Between the end of the Blackhawk Wars in 1832 and its statehood in 1848, the population of Wisconsin ballooned from 10,000 to 300,000, with many of the new settlers from New England and, in particular, upstate New York—enough to bring the sensibility of hops growing to establish a cottage industry. Moreover, growing hops in Wisconsin keenly made sense as, starting in the 1850s, Milwaukee and St. Louis became the primary hubs for German immigrants and, soon after, the top producing American breweries. Through the Civil War, Wisconsin became the leading producer for hops; by 1867, Wisconsin was producing 75 percent of hops grown in America.

About this same time, hops growing in Oregon matured from hobby growers to commercially oriented fields, laying the groundwork for what would be big business in the late nineteenth century. In 1869, George Leasure planted the first commercially successful hops fields in Lane County, smack in the middle of the Willamette Valley; soon after, other farmers followed. By the turn of the century, hops growing is the leading agricultural industry in the Willamette Valley, and by this point in history, the West Coast had fully taken over the industry, including robust crops in California, Oregon, Washington and eventually Idaho.

A Pioneering History

Rows of hops. *Oregon Hops & Beer Archives.*

Buoyed by the rising tide of beer drinking throughout America, the demand for hops also rose. In part, that growing market contributed to the growth of Oregon's hops industries; but more pressing, over the next three decades, three distinct factors established Oregon as the leading hops grower in the world.

First, the transcontinental railroad reached the West Coast in 1880. The lush farm fields of the Willamette Valley had been settled over the previous generation and were producing watermelons, almonds and apples—more than enough for the population of the Northwest—and were being shipped across America. Likewise, from 1870 to 1890, hops production in Oregon boomed from 9,745 pounds in 1870 to 244,371 in 1880 and then by another multiple of 15 to 3,811,320 pounds in 1890.

Within this industry, Southern Oregon was a secondary provider for hops, with particularly productive clusters around Grants Pass and the Applegate Valley—many of the same fields that today grow marijuana plants. In 1888, seventy thousand pounds of hops were shipped from Josephine County, according to the book *History of Josephine County* by Jack Sutton.

By 1890, there were an estimated two thousand growers in Oregon. Many were small plots, what would today be called "boutique." In 1916, even Governor Oswald West, who supported Prohibition and signed the statewide ban on beer into law, managed a small hops farm. There were only thirteen hops farms in Josephine County, a number slightly higher than the number of breweries in Southern Oregon at the time, but those farms were moderately large tracts—90 to 150 acres—and growing hyper-productive hops clusters. The group of hops farms in Josephine and Jackson Counties were large and organized enough to form their own trade association, the

Southern Oregon Hop Growers Association, separate from the Willamette Hop Growers Association.

The next opportunity for growth in Oregon's hops industry was a marketing coup. In 1905, Portland hosted the Lewis and Clark Centennial Exposition; much like a world fair (although not formally sanctioned as such), the event was a massive party that highlighted the wonders of the world, such as marble statues from Europe, blimp excursions and locally grown commodities like lumber and hops. Over the summer months, more than 2.5 million people attended, a remarkable number considering the entire state population of Oregon at the time was 413,000. As a direct result, the population of Portland nearly doubled from 1905 to 1910, from 161,000 to 270,000, growth mainly attributed to the fair. Likewise, between 1900 and 1906, hops production enjoyed yet another massive jump, nearly doubling over six years from 15,330,000 pounds in 1900 to 23,985,000 in 1906, the year after the Lewis and Clark Exposition.

It would seem logical that Prohibition would grind this production to a halt. Wheat and barley were grown in eastern Oregon, but those crops

Women working in hops fields. *Oregon Hops & Beer Archives.*

were somewhat immune to restrictions on beer production, as they have a multitude of other applications, while hops is a fairly specific product. But the early Oregon hops industry was largely structured on exports—first, to breweries throughout North America and, after World War I began, throughout the globe. Consider that in 1913, although Oregon produced 47 percent of hops marketed and sold in America, only 2 percent were consumed within the state's borders.

When Prohibition locked down breweries in Oregon in 1916, there was little impact, if any, on the hops growing industry, and by the time that Prohibition spread across the entire nation in 1919, Oregon hops growers had broken into a new, massive market: Europe.

When what is now known as World War I broke out in 1914, fierce battles raged throughout the European continent, leaving centuries-old fields trampled and scorched. Coupled with strict restrictions on nonessentials like beer, the hops industry in Europe, and particularly Germany, was laid to waste.

"A nicely timed war," quipped Tiah Edmunson-Morton, a curator at the Oregon Hops and Brewing Archives centered at Oregon State University. Edmunson-Morton went on to explain that in the early twentieth century, European hops had been considered superior, either by reality or simply by conceit. "Scrub weed" is a term she said was used for West Coast hops at the time, adding, "But it grew like gangbusters."

When World War I ended in 1918, Europeans were buying shiploads of Oregon "scrub weed" to continue to brew their beers—and that foothold in the market holds. From 1919 to 1933, hops acreage doubled in Oregon, and production tripled. By 1922, the hops industry from Josephine County was producing one million pounds, loading thirteen train car loads to European countries. That means that only one out of every twenty pounds of hops grown in Oregon at the time was being produced in Josephine County, which as a portion of the hops industry in Oregon isn't massive but as a stand-alone amount isn't a hill of beans. Consider that in 2018, Oregon produced one million pounds of marijuana, the same weight that Josephine County produced for hops in the 1920s.

Several collections provide insight into and information about the workforce that supported this industry, including the treasure-trove of photos and documents stored at OSU. One contemporary source of information about the workforce in the hops fields comes from a 1917 senior thesis, "History of Present Status of the Oregon Hop Industry," by a University of Oregon student, Karl Becke. Much like marijuana growing in the twenty-

Hops farm in Josephine County. *SOHS #09846.*

first century, hops is largely a seasonal affair, with massive populations of laborers—temporary pickers and migrant workers—swarming into the farms. In his thesis, Becke reports that starting on February 1, 1917, three thousand men were steadily employed for six months in the hops fields and industry; then, starting on September 1, fifty to sixty thousand people were employed for four weeks. That is a massive number, larger than the current population of Grants Pass and Ashland combined and, at the time, roughly equal to one-twelfth the entire population of Oregon.

The hops pickers came from all over and were a mix. A photograph at the Oregon Historical Society labeled "Josephine County hop farm," presumably from the 1910s, shows a Victorian-style farmhouse in the foreground and canvas tents pitched in a side yard, presumably for the growers, and exhibits the transient nature of the pickers. The photographs from the time also provide insight into who was picking—women in wide-brimmed hats and dresses, Grande Ronde Native Americans in full headdresses, Mexican workers, Chinese laborers and children.

One particular window into the world of hops fields—and an entertaining recommended side read—is a report primarily focused on the young women picking hops in Oregon. Written by Annie MacLean and published in 1909 by the University of Chicago Press, "With Oregon Hop

Hops! *Oregon Hops & Brewing Archives.*

Tiah Edmunson-Morton, archivist for Oregon Hops and Brewing. *Courtesy of Tiah Edmunson-Morton.*

Reportedly the largest beer can and bottle collection in Oregon, located at Caldera Brewing Co. *Author photo.*

Caldera was the first craft brewery to sell its beer in cans on the West Coast. *Courtesy of Caldera Brewing Co.*

Cameron Litton hangs out in the brewing room at Walkabout Brewing. *Courtesy of Cameron Litton.*

Taps at Walkabout Brewery. *Author photo.*

Talk about on ice—Southern Oregon Brewers Hockey league. *Rodney Rampy.*

Constructed in 1856, one of the first breweries in southern Oregon, the rather demure-looking Eagle Brewery still stands today in Jacksonville. *Author photo.*

Behind the scenes at Caldera Brewery. *Author photo*.

Built in 1902 as the Grants Pass Brewery, a century later this building houses Climate City Brewery. *Author photo*.

Left: A former automotive sales room is now Common Block, a bustling brewpub in downtown Medford. *Courtesy of Common Block Brewing.*

Middle: Summertime at Common Block Brewing. *Courtesy of Common Block Brewing.*

Bottom: A plaque on the side of Climate City Brewing announces what first stood there. *Author photo.*

The collection of growlers at Opposition Brewery in Medford. *Author photo*.

A flight of beers at Osmo's in Medford. *Nick Blakeslee*.

Caldera was the first to can craft beer on the West Coast. Waiting for shipment. *Author photo*.

Above: Six bottles on the Wild River Pizza wall. *Courtesy of Wild River Pizza.*

Left: Rows of hops. *Oregon Hops & Beer Archives.*

Left: Fresh hops. *Oregon Hops & Beer Archives.*

Below: A favorite in Ashland, but sadly a casualty of closures, Swing Tree Brewing. *Courtesy of the* Rogue Valley Messenger.

Above: Brewing tanks at Klamath Basin Brewing in Klamath Falls. *Courtesy of Klamath Basin Brewing.*

Right: Beer brewed at Conner Fields is served at The Haul in Grants Pass. *Courtesy of Jon Conner/Conner Fields.*

Flight at Portal Brewing. *Nick Blakeslee.*

Flight at Opposition Brewing. *Nick Blakeslee.*

Above: Flight at Wild River Pizza. *Nick Blakeslee.*

Left: Yoga and beer, a relaxing pair at Walkabout Brewing. *Courtesy of Cameron Litton.*

Above: Klamath Basin Brewing in Klamath Falls. *Courtesy of Klamath Basin Brewing.*

Left: Theresa Delaney, co-owner for Portal Brewery, estimates she has hand painted more than one thousand growlers for Portal's patrons. *Courtesy of Theresa Delaney.*

Right: The Haul in Grants Pass. *Nick Blakeslee.*

Below: Caldera is the largest brewpub and largest distributor in southern Oregon. *Courtesy of Caldera Brewing Co.*

Above: A working farm and a tasting room, Conner Fields supplies beer for The Haul in Grants Pass. *Courtesy of Jon Conner/Conner Fields.*

Left: Although better known for wine growing, Conner Fields has begun growing hops in the Applegate Valley and also brewing beer. *Courtesy of Jon Conner/Conner Fields.*

Two young women picking and loading hops. *Oregon Hops & Beer Archives.*

Pickers" details the pickers' lifestyles. Ultimately, MacLean only spent a day picking hops and an overnight in the camps, but her observations bring to life the characters and terrain from this era and lifestyle, from the train station where carloads of workers boarded to the conversations women exchanged on the picking rows. A century later, MacLean is considered a pioneer in sociology, and in 1910, she published a far-reaching study, *Wage-Earning Women*, which employed a staff of twenty-nine women sociologists surveying hundreds of American companies. Her observations and notes from the hops fields read like a smart, albeit slightly aloof, journal from a day in the life.

Like marijuana "clippers" decades later, the hops-picking workforce worked in a cash industry—and the rates are and were lousy. In 1933, in the thick of the Great Depression, workers earned one penny for every pound of hops picked—roughly $1.50 for a hearty day's work picking 150 pounds. Even by the bleak standards of the day, that pay is about one-third the national average. But it was readily available cash.

By 1940, wages had not improved much: three cents per pound. During the World War II years, wages skyrocketed to nearly ten dollars per day, exceeding national averages, although the work was seasonal, and by this time, most farms were increasingly relying on mechanical picking and the demand for pickers was waning.

Farms in Southern Oregon, however, continued with the more human labor-intensive practices, parallel to national trends for family farms in the middle of the twentieth century; soon, the industry began to consolidate into larger, more efficient and mechanized farms.

By the 1960s, there were only five hops growers remaining in Josephine County, including the two largest: Mel King, who managed 130 acres, and the Lathrop Farm, with 230 acres. A 1965 report from a USDA hops researcher, Dr. Al Haunold, provides a postcard of information. "Grant Pass is located in a rather small valley in Southern Oregon and hop growing competed with other agricultural activities, primarily fruit growing," he writes. "I remember Chuck Lathrop mentioning occasionally that he had gotten offers for his land from an adjoining pear operation and also from a poultry operation nearby."

Over the next decade, even those last hops farmers in Southern Oregon surrendered to market pressures—and hops production in Oregon concentrated in Willamette Valley, primarily clustered around Independence. Oregon remained a top provider, but Washington surpassed the state as the number-one hops grower and provider—and continues to dominate the industry today.

In 1989, Sunny Brooks Hops Farm closed. It was the last hops farm in Josephine County in the twentieth century. At the time, there was only one independent brewery in Southern Oregon: Rogue Ales had opened two years earlier in Ashland—although the bulk of its production was on the coast in Newport. Likewise, the number of breweries in America has shrunk, with several breweries controlling 90 percent of beer production—and, notably, contracting with a select number of large, industrialized hops farms and brokers.

But starting in 2008, Standing Stone Brewery in Ashland forged a collaboration with Hanley Farm to buy locally grown, organic and heritage hops. Hanley Farm is owned by Southern Oregon Historical Society. A contemporary article in the *Medford Mail Tribune* announced that Hanley would plant one hundred hops plants—enough, said Alex Amarotico, to provide about 10 percent needed at the brewery.

In part, explained Amarotico, the project was motivated by rising hops costs. "The price has tripled in the last year and a half," lamented Amarotico in the article. "When I started brewing in '97, we were paying $4 a pound. We're paying about $25 a pound now."

Furthermore, Standing Stone Brewery has pushed a mission for sustainability, taking the unique step to draft a mission statement, much like a nonprofit would do. That philosophy has led the brewery to pulling ingredients for its food and beer from as close to Ashland as possible.

The year after Hanley Farm planted hops, a family farm near Ashland also started to grow and harvest hops—organically, without pesticides or fertilizers, a rare practice in the hops industry. When sap-suck insects attacked the plants that year, the farm countered with ladybugs—and, at the end of the summer, Hanley was able to harvest enough to sell seventy-five pounds of hops each to Caldera Brewing Co. and Standing Stone Brewery. It may not have been enough hops to supply all the new breweries in the region, but it was a beginning.

5
1933-1996

Prohibition Ends, Homebrew Clubs and Brewpubs

In 1932, Franklin D. Roosevelt campaigned for president on a platform that included repealing the Volstead Act, the hulking legislation that had shut down the manufacture of beer, wine and liquor for the previous fifteen years. In part, FDR advocated, beer and liquor sales would tap a steady flow of much-needed tax revenue. At the other podium, his opponent, the incumbent and Oregon-raised Herbert Hoover, had supported Prohibition, going so far as to call it "the great social and economic experiment, noble in motive and far reaching in purpose."

In 1933, Congress amended the Volstead Act and, ultimately, repealed Prohibition. Within twenty-four hours of re-legalization, 1.5 million barrels of beer were sold. A line a mile long stretched from the front doors at the Anheuser-Busch plant in St. Louis. At the White House, reportedly, the new president celebrated with his favorite drink, a dirty martini, and had a six pack of beer delivered to him by a police officer.

All told, 756 breweries whirred back to life, about half the number in operation before Prohibition. The hundreds of breweries that did not reopen were regional breweries, like Marie Kienlen's Grants Pass Brewery, although some did come off mothballs, like a Klamath Falls brewery, which returned in 1933 but closed again in a heartbeat. Conversely, all of the larger players—Anheuser-Busch, Schlitz, Miller and, in Oregon, the Portland-based Weinhard—did reopen. Over the next few decades, the number of breweries in America steadily declined to 468 in 1945, 229 in 1960 and 154 in 1970, as beer production was constricted to a few major breweries.

Many of the breweries financially survived fifteen years of Prohibition by selling soda pops, including Hamm's in Minnesota, Weinhard's well-liked root beer and cream soda in Portland and Marie's Grants Pass Brewery; although, she was seventy-four when Prohibition ended and didn't reopen her brewery. Busch used its refrigerated truck to transport ice cream during Prohibition years, and Pabst diversified, transforming its warehouses into cold storage for cheese and also producing malt syrup, which was marketed as an ingredient for baking cookies but was, of course, known to be used for homebrewing.

Although beer was once again "legal" in 1933, there were important limitations. At first, Congress only allowed 3.2 percent beer, until the Twenty-First Amendment was adopted in December. Moreover, no direct distribution from manufacturer to consumer was allowed—a restriction that would crimp Oregon's beer industry for five more decades. While Marie sold buckets of beer for a quarter at her Grants Pass brewery, that sort of direct-to-consumer sale would not be replicated again in Oregon until brewpubs and growler stations were again legalized in the 1980s.

Even so, while those restrictions shaped the production and distribution of beer through the next few decades, they didn't slow beer sales too much. Even though Prohibition ended in the thick of the Depression, beer sales were so brisk in the few days following the repeal of Prohibition that the federal government earned $10 million in taxes and pushed alcohol into the position of the third-largest federal revenue source, after income and cigarette taxes.

Although most of the small breweries in America did not survive fifteen years without beer sales, one of the more successful post-Prohibition stories began when the Southern Oregon Brewery reopened. The facility had sold to Portland-based Weinhard in 1897 and was largely converted to an ice production facility. But by the 1930s, the ice business was waning as electricity for home appliances rapidly expanded.

In 1914, a Detroit engineer invented a home refrigerator, and four years later, just as Prohibition was locking down breweries and pushing breweries like the Medford Brewing Company to rely on making ice to replace the revenue lost from the lack of beer sales, the Frigidaire Company began to mass-produce home refrigerators. During the fifteen years of Prohibition, households filled up with mass-marketed inventions like automobiles, vacuum cleaners, washing machines and refrigerators. They became commonplace. Between the beginning and end of Prohibition, refrigerators went from nearly nonexistent in American households to an appliance in roughly half of American homes. Correspondingly, icehouses like the Medford Brewing Company were quickly becoming as obsolete as horses and buggies.

In 1933, a locally based investor group purchased the facility in Medford back from the Portland owners and, with slight modifications, retooled the brewery to triple its capacity, reopening under the original name, the Southern Oregon Brewery. Following successful branding like Pabst Blue Ribbon, which had ruled the national market since 1844 with its self-dubbed claim as the "blue ribbon" winner, the Medford-based brewery released Gold Seal and Gold Seal Bock; their third brand, Old Rogue Lager, boasted a bit more regional flair and pride.

Although beer consumption continued to rise in years after Prohibition ended, that trend did not benefit the Southern Oregon Brewery, as 82 percent of the beer consumed in Oregon at the time was produced out of state.

Five years later, Southern Oregon Brewery had a shake-up, changing its general manager to Bill Chrysler and rebranding as A-One Brewery. Likewise, it released a new flagship beer, A-1. Hardly a novel name, A-1 has been in wide use for products for a century, probably most notably for the steak sauce, which has been trademarked in America since 1831. The A-One Brewery released a second line of beers: The Old King Cole, so named for a seventeenth-century nursery rhyme in which a commoner becomes the king—and his first order of business is to call for his pipe, bowl and musicians, with the "bowl" being a drinking vessel. The name "Old King Cole" was keenly in the zeitgeist at the time, the subject for an early Disney cartoon and, a few years later, as the plot for a Three Stooges movie.

To supplement revenue from beer sales, the A-One Brewery borrowed a business strategy from Prohibition and turned to soda pop production. It released two flavors, Mission Orange and a ginger ale called Clicquot Club. Both flavors were well-known national lines of soda pop, and it isn't clear whether A-One franchised those flavors or was simply wildcatting, producing counterfeit sodas. There are no records available that support either theory, only conjecture.

What makes the approved production of the two sodas improbable is that the flavors were from two separate, competing companies. Moreover, neither company was headquartered within one thousand miles from Medford, and without the internet to monitor trademark violations, the possibility for free use of a trademark was as unchecked as a Bangkok street marketplace.

Clicquot Club was a Massachusetts-based company and one of the best-selling sodas in the country. It was an innovative company that, in 1893, was the first to put a metal cap on a bottle. In the 1920s, Clicquot Club had pursued massive advertisement campaigns, including an animated sign in Times Square (the largest animated sign in the world from 1924 to 1926) and sponsored a musical variety radio show. Why would it need to contract with a small brewery in Southern Oregon? Moreover, much of the success for Clicquot Club's ginger ale was based on its use of particular ingredients. Would the company really ship those specific gingers and sugars across the country to Medford?

However, arguing for the viability of the idea that the A-One Brewery was legitimately producing the ginger ale, in 1938, Clicquot Club set up a dozen or so factories coast-to-coast. The timing synchs with A-One Brewery's launch of Clicquot Club soda, an idea also underscored by the reality that much of the success for Clicquot Club had been based on its reliance on railroads for distribution—and the A-One Brewery was directly across the street from a busy station.

The second line of soda pop A-One Brewery began to produce was Mission Orange, another popular brand name of the era. Produced by a Los Angeles company, Mission Orange was an early adopter of product placement in movies.

Ultimately, the Medford-based brewery survived fifteen years, bootstrapping itself out of the Depression era only to be drained by World War II, a global event that was pivotal in the domestic beer industry. While beer production increased by more than 50 percent during the four years American troops fought in Europe and the Pacific, that rising tide did not benefit all breweries. Instead, what benefitted the larger breweries crushed many of the small and regional breweries that were still trying to establish a market after Prohibition.

For starters, the outbreak of World War II provided a fresh opportunity to propose Prohibition, an idea still popular with a sizable portion of Americans. Once again, there were lobbying efforts to ban beer, with the argument that the wheat used for production would be better spent producing bread and cereals for the troops and space on cargo shipments for beer better used for weapons or food supplies.

Lobbyists from the beer companies and the newly merged United States Brewer Association countered that brewer's yeast offered health benefits from its vitamin B and would help fortify troops—an argument that eventually won the debate. As a concession, though, breweries were taxed heavily, with 15 percent of their production dedicated for "military use."

Moreover, the rations on wheat during the war years disproportionately favored the large breweries like Anheuser-Busch, which could swap out wheat and barley with rice without much affecting the taste or heft of the

A Pioneering History

lightweight pilsners. On the contrary, the smaller-batch lagers had a more difficult time masking the changes, although the Salem Brewery Association tried to counter these changes and simultaneously capitalize on the groundswell of homegrown patriotism with brand names like Victory Beer.

Interestingly, in spite of anti-German sentiment that swept across America, this attitude did not seem to touch breweries, which still very much advertised their German heritage through their very brand names. By the end of 1942, production of beer by Anheuser-Busch exceeded three million barrels for the first time—and only continued to expand production during the subsequent years.

More generally, World War II served as a catalyst for trends in the beer industry: Even though production of beer rose from 1940 to 1945 by more than 50 percent, from fifty-five to eighty-six million gallons—and Americans are individually consuming 50 percent more beer and alcohol by the end of the war, more than eighteen gallons each year—the number of individual breweries continued to plummet. While there were 684 breweries at the beginning of the war, by the end there were only 468 remaining.

A-One Brewery survived the four years of World War II, and in 1945, General Manager Bill Chrysler took over and, one more time, renamed the company, this time to Chrystal Brewing, not quite his last name, but more or less after himself, presumably as there was already a famous car company with his precise name.

But the beer—and its soda pop—failed. In 1947, the facility closed, leaving only two breweries in Oregon at the time, the Salem-based Sicks' Brewing Company and the merged company of Blitz-Weinhard in Portland. In 1953, the Salem brewery closed.

Beyond the immediate production costs and various restrictions on the supply side, the four years of World War II profoundly impacted the demand for beer, with an entire generation—or, at least tens of thousands of coming-of-age servicemen—weaned on lightweight pilsners; certainly, it was a major contributing factor. By 1950, ten breweries were responsible for 38 percent of the beer consumed in America, and there wasn't much breadth in the spectrum

Chrystal Beer, a final attempt for the Medford brewery to stay open, 1945. *Oregon Historical Society*.

of taste those breweries offered. Moreover, already a sizable portion, that market slice grew to nearly the entire pie by 1980, when the ten largest brewers controlled 93 percent of the market. In particular, Anheuser-Busch. Miller also leapfrogged up the charts, starting as the tenth-largest brewery in America in 1960, notching up slightly to seventh in 1970 and then reaching number two in 1980, largely fueled by the success of its Miller Lite beer and a massive media blitz that featured the likes of manly men like Joe Frazier, decked in a tux and fur coat, sashaying into a ritzy bar with his Miller Lite. The image helped normalize even the burliest men drinking beer that has as few calories as it does flavor and gave the market a big shove away from flavorful, unique beers.

Mirroring the hold that the big breweries had on the American public, it is not coincidental that *Laverne & Shirley* was the most-watched TV show in America in 1977 and 1978, featuring a storyline that follows two mildly goofy roommates in Milwaukee, Wisconsin, who work on the bottling line at the fictitious Shotz Brewery, a certain stand-in for Schlitz, which was second only to Anheuser-Busch until 1976, the year before the show debuted.

During these decades, though, there were several important countertrends that set the stage for the modern-day craft beer and small brewery renaissance. Interestingly, in the 1950s and '60s, Ballantine introduced the first real IPA to America. With 7.9 percent ABV, the beer would fit well with the current trend of bold and bombastic IPAs, but at the time, it was outlandish. Even so, the IPA grabbed beer drinkers' attention and imagination, and Ballantine was the third-largest brewery in America in 1950. By 1960, Ballatine had slipped to sixth and, soon after, completely fell off the charts, leaving the beer market dominated by the light pilsners like Budweiser and Pabst Blue Ribbon.

Even so, Ballatine rooted something in the American taste buds, and survived until 1996. Moreover, about the same time that Ballatine began to slip from popular tastes, an heir to the Maytag fortune, Fritz Maytag, purchased a flagging San Francisco brewery, Anchor Brewing Company. With roots reaching back to a German brewer who arrived during the California gold rush, Anchor Brewing Company was one of the few—if not only—remaining "steam brewers," a process that incorporates lager ingredients with techniques more associated with making ales.

Without adequate sources of ice or refrigeration, many turn-of-the-century San Francisco brewers pumped in the cool Pacific Ocean breezes and the city's famous fog to cool their brews. As both the yeast and the fermentation temperature influence the beer's flavor, steam beer is unique from—but also similar to—both ales and lagers, in that it uses lager yeast but ferments at a temperature more associated with ales. The result is a distinct, slightly bifurcated flavor—part sour ale, part easygoing lager.

Maytag purchased 51 percent of the brewery for a few thousand dollars, and by 1971, Anchor was producing the flagship Anchor Steam—which, in turn, like so many aspects of San Francisco, became a beacon for a culture counter to the mainstream trends.

A few years later, and forty miles north over the Golden Gate Bridge, what is known as the country's first craft brewery, the New Albion Brewing Company, opened. Started by Jack McAuliffe, the company was inspired by his experiences while in the U.S. Navy and stationed in Scotland, where he sampled all sorts of beers no longer available in America and, eventually, pieced together his own homebrewing kit. When he returned stateside and was working as an optical engineer in what is now known as Silicon Valley, McAuliffe was inspired by Maytag's Anchor Brewing Company and went about figuring out how to expand his homebrew hobby into a full-fledged brewery.

But unable to afford San Francisco's rents, he relocated to Sonoma, a region more associated with zinfandels than hops and, with a nod to history, named the brewery the New Albion Brewing Company, after what explorer Francis Drake had called the San Francisco Bay area, as well as a former San Francisco brewery. Production was small, about seven and a half gallons per week, close to what Schutz was brewing in Jacksonville a century earlier. But with its unique pale ales, porters and stouts, the brewery found widespread fame in the *New York Times* and *Washington Post*. Even so, the brewery couldn't make ends meet and closed in 1982 after six years—after inspiring other homebrewers to open their own businesses, most notably Sierra Nevada Brewing Company, which is now the country's seventh-largest brewery, and Mendocino Brewing Company, which opened the first brewpub in America. In her 2006 book, *Ambitious Brew: The Story of American Beer*, Maureen Ogle calls the New Albion Brewing Company "the most important failed brewery in the industry's history."

With these changes percolating, another important opportunity was uncorked: In 1978, homebrewing was "legalized" in America. As an odd oversight, when Prohibition was lifted, homebrewing beer essentially remained illegal (although making wine at home was legalized).

Eliminating—or at least banning—homebrewing eliminated an important training ground for potential new brewers for decades. Of course, it did not mean that no one was homebrewing, just as plenty of people in Southern Oregon grew a few marijuana plants in their backyards or on their windowsills before legalization. By the 1970s, homebrewing was beginning to take tentative steps into the mainstream, like a 1970 book by Portland-based Fred Eckhardt, *A Treatise on Lager Beers*, which provides the know-how to brew your own beers. For the previous several years, Eckhardt had been teaching homebrewing classes in Oregon. And a few years later, the first acknowledged homebrewing club formed in Los Angeles, the Maltose Falcons.

The change is important to understand, as 90 percent of the pioneering brewers in the late 1970s and 1980s claimed to have started as homebrewers, including McAuliffe with New Albion Brewing Company and a batch of new brewers who started the first new breweries in Southern Oregon in the 1990s—Jim Mills, with Caldera Brewery; Ross Litton, an Australian plumber who started Walkabout Brewery in Medford; and Hubert Smith, who brought a line of award-winning craft beers to Wild River Pizza in Grants Pass.

Before 1978, though, most homebrewing was something akin to bands of rebel warriors gathering in garages and basements across America. As there weren't any retail stores dedicated to homebrewing kits and supplies, cobbling together a mini home brewery required trips to the hardware store.

The result from legalizing homebrewing was the beginning to what has been called the "beer revolution"—a moment that established a training ground and ushered in an army of new brewers, breweries and beer styles. It was as if watercolors and paint brushes had been banned for decades for home use; suddenly, there was an explosion of reds, blues and yellows as new artists tried out their hands. It took a few years for those homebrewers to translate to bigger plans, but by the mid-1980s, momentum was swinging away from the consolidation of the beer industry.

In 1980, there were only forty-four breweries remaining in America. But a decade after homebrewing was legalized, nearly two hundred new craft breweries had opened—although a quick and healthy growth, it was dwarfed by what happened in the following decade.

Legalizing homebrewing vastly widened the spectrum for beer flavors and styles and opened the door to tens of thousands of men and women to experiment, testing the basics of beer brewing before scaling to a full-fledged brewery—an allowance that, even decades later, continues to usher in hundreds more brewers. For Opposition Brewery in Medford, one of Southern Oregon's newer breweries, which started in 2012, the initial spark was a homebrew kit bought on a whim. As Nick Ellis, one of the co-owners, tells the story, he and his wife were bored one weekend. In the economic

Nick Ellis started homebrewing on a whim and later started Opposition Brewery. *Author photo*.

downturn of 2008, Ellis had been laid off from a position at Southern Oregon University. "We were window shopping at Blackbird," Ellis explained, referring to a catch-all hardware and hobby store in Medford. "I told my wife that I didn't know how to make anything. I couldn't weld. No woodworking." Somewhat impulsively, he bought a five-gallon bucket and #5 can of syrup, as Ellis tells the story, standing in the warehouse bunker that serves as their brewery and taproom. The clientele is loud, and everyone seems to know everyone else's name, to borrow a tagline. There are dart boards and ring-toss games. While Ellis was talking about his start in brewing, his dog Charlie wandered into the back room, and without looking at the dog, Ellis leaned over to scratch behind his ears. Ellis's first batch, he says, was "drinkable." Over the next few months, he began to improve his skills, storing thirty-gallon "pots" in his garage—and soon after, Ellis and his wife paired with another couple to start their brewery: a story, and brewery, that wouldn't have happened had homebrewing still been illegal.

A good deal of credit for lifting the ban on homebrewing has been given to President Jimmy Carter, who signed into law H.R. 1337. But that credit oversimplifies and ignores the deeper machinations that brought about the change. For starters, President Carter, a Baptist and a reputed teetotaler, did not introduce the bill, he simply signed it into law in October 1977.

His brother, on the other hand, had earned a reputation as the black sheep and, more specifically, as one of the most iconic beer drinkers of the mid-'70s—his well-publicized choice drink being Pabst Blue Ribbon, until an entire beer line, Billy Beer, was introduced in 1977. Some accounts have glibly attributed that it was the influence of Billy Carter that softened his older brother to the idea for legalizing homebrewing; but again, that is misplaced, although the timing is certainly suspect, with Billy Beer being introduced in the summer of 1977 and his older brother signing into law H.R. 1337 in October 1978.

But Billy Beer really had nothing to do with homebrewing and, instead, was a marketing ploy by a Louisville-based company, Falls City Brewery, which had existed since 1905. The company was relatively successful and even prospered during Prohibition with ice production and a soda pop line still profitable into the 1970s. No stranger to publicity and publicity stunts, the Falls Brewery had been the official beer for the Indianapolis 500 in the 1930s and sponsored NASCAR racers through the decades. In an effort to shore up declining sales against the onslaught of the national breweries, in 1977, Falls City approached Billy Carter, a notorious Pabst Blue Ribbon drinker. The brewery presented a few different flavors, and he chose one, endorsing the beer with the motto, "It's the best beer I've ever tasted, and I've tasted a lot."

Propped up by an extensive marketing campaign, the beer was an overnight sensation, but it lacked an important quality: It wasn't very good and became a blink-of-the-eye fad, with the cost of the marketing campaign and rapid decline in sales gutting the company. A year later, the Falls City Brewery sold to the Wisconsin-based Neileman Brewing Company, which in turn was gobbled up by Stroh's in 1996.

If anything, Billy Beer was an ill-conceived attempt by a regional brewery to break into the national market and to do so with a beer as plain and unimaginative as the contemporary macrobrews; it was not a scrappy homebrew exploring new frontiers in the beer market.

Moreover—and probably more to the point—the bill wasn't introduced by Jimmy Carter. He signed the bill, which tucked the homebrewer allowances in among four other amendments and changes to the tax code, including more routine considerations on tax considerations for trust rollovers and Social Security cash payouts. (Notably, the bill also allowed any adult to homebrew, as opposed to previous allowances for only "the head of a family.") Credit for lifting the cloud over homebrewers, instead, should go to a second-term U.S. senator from California, Alan Cranston—and even then, it was a small group of constituents who had lobbied him to introduce the tax code change, primarily Lee Coe, a Californian and member of the Maltose Falcons, a LA-based homebrewing group, and Nancy Crosby, another Maltose Falcon and head for a trade group supporting home-winemaking shops.

But lifting the ban on homebrewing only removed one of two major obstacles. The second was a ban on brewpubs.

After Prohibition was lifted in 1933, federal lawmakers instilled a few safeguards to regulate alcohol production and consumption. The ban on homebrewing was one. Another was a more general, and generally well intended, notion to prevent monopolies by separating beer and alcohol producers from direct distribution and sale.

In the decades before Prohibition, venues like the Jacksonville breweries that hosted beer gardens, and certainly breweries like Marie Kienlen's Grants Pass Brewery that sold buckets of beer to anyone who stopped by, were free-for-alls. Often called "tied houses," they also were the bane for pro-Prohibitionists and the temperance movement, as this system allowed for brewers to maintain lower prices—and, presumably, more drinking.

With such experiences still fresh in lawmakers' minds, the result was a three-tier system in which producers (tier one) sold to independent middlemen that were wholesalers or distributors (tier two), who then sold to retailers (tier three). Effectively, the three-tier system provided more opportunity for regulation over beer and alcohol and was intended to weaken individual breweries' hold on the market. However, in effect, outlawing so-called tied houses—or in more contemporary speak, brewpubs or public houses—favored bigger breweries. The problem was outlawing brewpubs widened the gap between brewers and consumers, a problem particularly keen for smaller breweries who didn't have plump marketing budgets and sufficient staff to oversee distribution strategies. Also, prohibiting brewpubs forced breweries to bottle or can, as opposed to selling on-site draft, yet another expense and advantage to big breweries like Anheuser-Busch and Miller. Not to mention, the big breweries often pressured distributors to carry their beers exclusively, locking out any new competition.

For five decades, these restrictions closed an entry point to the market for small local breweries. But the laws were left to state legislatures to enforce, and by 1982, homebrewers in California and Washington both successfully rolled back the restrictions on tied houses and opened the first brewpubs in the nation—including what is roundly considered the first modern-day brewpub in America, the Yakima Brewing and Malting Co., which was opened by a fifty-four-year-old Scottish brewer in an old opera house in the heart of hops country in northeast Washington. (The brewer, Bert Grant, had been around the beer business since the age of ten and knew that beer existed beyond Budweiser and Pabst Blue Ribbon. The first batch of beer from Yakima Brewing was, fittingly, a Scottish Ale; the second was a little-known-at-the-time India Pale Ale. Many attribute the current popularity for IPAs to Grant and also credit him with introducing the Cascade hops to dozens of other influential brewers.)

A year later, Mendocino Brewing opened in the appropriately named small town of Hopland in northern California. It was the second brewpub in America and the first in California.

Like the more recent legalization of marijuana in nearby states, the successes in Washington and California inspired others to push for legislative changes. By 1984, a group of entrepreneurs and wannabe brewers in Oregon had cooked up the idea to present a brewpub bill to the state legislature. Many of the names and breweries are now familiar: Kurt and Rob Widmer, Mike and Brian McMenamin and Dick and Nancy Ponzi. The Ponzis already operated Ponzi Vineyards, and in 1984, they opened Columbia River Brewing (later renamed Bridgeport) and hoped to apply the idea of tasting rooms to their brewery, a concept that has served wineries well (and had been legalized for wineries years earlier).

With stars in their eyes, the group of up-and-coming brewery owners drafted legislation to permit brewpubs and cajoled a state representative into introducing House Bill 2284. At first, everything went swimmingly. HB 2284 sailed through the Oregon House untouched by controversy or opposition; it passed 56–0.

But HB 2284 sank in the state senate. Providing a quick lesson in politics, on April 11, 1985, Dick Ponzi delivered his arguments to the Oregon Senate's Business, Housing and Finance Committee. It was the same logic and testimony that worked in the House. But three weeks later, on May 9, the bill was tabled by Senator L.B. Day (R-Salem) in a work committee, which effectively means that the bill would not see the light of day again. It seems as if Day had a strong political supporter in his district who owned a beer distribution company and believed that brewpubs and direct brewer-to-consumer distribution would hurt his bottom line.

With only a few weeks left in the legislative session, it looked like the Brew Pub Bill would need to wait for another year.

But politics is all about friends—and brewpubs received not one, but two, more opportunities. Supporters for the idea tucked language into two different bills that would allow for brewpubs. The first bill allowed for the sale of unpasteurized beer in retail outlets, and on June 4, Representative Verner Anderson (R-Roseburg) added language to another bill that allowed liquor licenses for bed-and-breakfasts—and it was this second bill that Trojan horsed brewpubs into Oregon. On July 13, 1985, Republican governor Vic Atiyeh signed the bill into law, ultimately giving a chance for small breweries to successfully open in the state.

Oddly, as a side story to the Brewpub Law, Coors became an odd bedfellow with the Oregon microbreweries and proposed brewpubs. It has often been reported that the brewpubs rode the coattails of Coors into the state; but in fact, that is not the case. Instead, yes, Coors was actively lobbying lawmakers to sell its beers in retail outlets for several years prior—and in June, after the Brew Pub Bill died in a work session, Senate Bill 45 picked up both language to allow brewpubs to operate and also for Coors (or, specifically, unpasteurized beer) to sell in retail outlets.

House approves Coors bill 45-14

By FOSTER CHURCH
of The Oregonian staff

SALEM — A bill that would allow Coors beer to be sold in Oregon stores passed the House Tuesday on a 45-14 vote. It was the first time legislation favoring Coors had passed either chamber.

The bill still requires Senate approval. But because of a procedural maneuver in committee, it will proceed directly to the Senate floor, bypassing a hostile Senate Labor Committee.

Senate Bill 45 contains two major features. One would allow non-pasteurized beers — Coors is the most notable example — to be sold in places other than bars and taverns.

The second part, usually called "brewpub" legislation, would allow breweries to open taverns on their premises and sell food and beer.

Opposition to sale of Coors has usually come from organized labor and other interests that object to the political and labor philosophies of the Colorado-based Coors family.

House debate focused on economic development issues, with little attention paid to the ideology of the Coors organization.

Rep. Al Young, D-Hillsboro, who carried the bill on the floor, said the question was whether Oregon was truly receptive to new business.

"Are we really open for business in Oregon?" he asked, adding that a vote against the bill would work to the advantage of special-interest groups.

The Oregon AFL-CIO has traditionally fought measures to benefit Coors, as have some organizations supporting women and minority rights.

Rep. Ron Cease, D-Portland, also supported the bill, adding that the issue was not whether Coors would be "a good corporate citizen," or whether sale of non-pasteurized beer would create health problems, but whether it should be sold in stores.

Cease said there was some indication that the company was changing some of its more controversial political policies, and he added that suggestions that unpasteurized beer can be unhealthful are false.

The original reason for limiting the sale of unpasteurized beer in cans and bottles in Oregon was a potential health danger. Coors now uses a filtration process that corporate officials say eliminates the need for pasteurization.

Rep. Mary Burrows, R-Eugene, was less enthusiastic in her support than Cease but said she also would vote for the bill.

Burrows said she disapproved of some of the reported political stands of corporate officials but added, "I don't intend to buy any, but I'm glad you're here."

The bill now goes directly to the floor of the Senate.

In the 1985 Oregon legislative session, Coors and craft beers made odd bedfellows. *Oregon Historical Newspaper database.*

In many states at the time, Coors was outright or partially banned, ostensibly because its beer is cold-filtered and not pasteurized, a process that some claimed promised health risks. The ban was so much a part of 1970s lore that *Time* magazine reported that President Gerald Ford kept an illicit stash of Coors in the White House refrigerator, and it was the central plot point for *Smokey and the Bandit*, the second-highest-grossing film in 1977 (to *Star Wars*), in which Burt Reynold's character is a truck driver trying to smuggle a truckload of Coors across state lines from Texas to Georgia. That is the sort of publicity that no advertising campaign could buy, and Coors held a certain outlaw lore and underdog reputation; after all, Coors was an American success story, as Adolph Coors was a German immigrant who was able to start a successful brewery in a small, western gold rush town (not completely unlike Veit Schutz).

But, of course, by the 1970s, Coors Brewing Company was no underdog. Joseph Coors, the grandson of founder Adolph Coors, took over as the company's president—and he actively used his wealth to fund ultraconservative political causes, including donating a plane for the Contras in Nicaragua. The company also began to lobby—often successfully—to undo restrictions against transporting toxic aluminum waste from can production across adjacent state borders, and several unfair labor practice lawsuits were filed against the company—by minorities, women and gay workers. And, probably most famously, in 1977, Coors broke a union strike by firing union workers and dismantling the union. That same year, in San Francisco, up-and-coming politician Harvey Milk scored his first major political victory—and eventually garnered support from unions—when he led a boycott of Coors in the gay bars in the city.

A Pioneering History

In Oregon, Coors was able to sell kegs and packaged beers in taverns, but that was a fraction of the available market—and Coors wanted more. In 1985, it sued the Oregon Liquor Control Commission to allow the sale of Coors in retail shops. Simultaneously, it submitted House Bill 2015 and, when that failed, added language to SB 45 allowing sales of unpasteurized beer in retail stores to allowances for brewpubs. Some of the same lobbyists opposing Coors were the same beer distributors standing against brewpubs, and Coors was able to soften that opposition, perhaps assisting brewpubs with their other bill. Even so, ultimately, SB 45 failed.

But quite literally hours after SB 45 failed, Coors scored a victory in its lawsuit when a circuit court judge in Portland ruled that unpasteurized beer possesses no health risks. A week later, the state legislature submitted yet another bill, Senate Bill 50, which specifically allows for the sale of unpasteurized beer in Oregon retail shops—and it passed.

On July 4, 1985, a convoy of trucks carrying Coors beer rolled over the California border into Ashland with the first shipments of cold-filtered, unpasteurized beers.

Three years after the Oregon legislature approved what is now known as the Brewpub Bill (even though it really pertained primarily to bed-and-breakfasts), the first brewpub opened in Southern Oregon. Located in a subterranean basement adjacent to Lithia Creek, the space was a cozy spot called Rogue Ales. More associated with the foggy and moody coastal town of Newport, Rogue Ales stuck around Ashland until 1996, but after its first year of operations in Ashland, Rogue had already relocated its main operations to a larger facility on the coast. As the story goes, a year after opening the brewpub in Ashland, the founder, Jack Joyce, was caught in an unlikely snowstorm on the coast and bumped into a woman, Mo, who owned Mo's Restaurants. She fed him a bowl of clam chowder and told him about her dream to live above a bar and said she knew of the perfect place. It just needed a tenant for the rest of the nearly two thousand square feet. Mo rented Joyce and Rogue Ale the space, with the condition that a photo of her in the bathtub would forever hang above the bar (it still does). By 2018, Rogue Ales had become the second-largest brewery in Oregon and the forty-second in the country.

Even though Rogue Ales didn't stick around Ashland for too long—and really did most of its growing elsewhere—the brewery in Ashland served as a starting point for brewpubs in Southern Oregon, as the first new brewery in Southern Oregon since Chrystal Brewery in Medford closed in 1947 and as a launching pad for two of the pioneers for modern-day breweries in Southern Oregon: Jim Mills with Caldera Brewing Co. and Ross Litton, who started Walkabout Brewery.

Shortly after Rogue Ales opened in Ashland, another brewpub opened near Grants Pass in 1990—and has stayed in operation ever since, making Wild River Pizza the longest-running brewpub in Southern Oregon.

What perhaps sets Wild River Pizza apart, though, is that most brewpubs start with the idea for a brewery and build a restaurant around the beer, as a means to draw in more customers and revenue; Wild River was the reverse. It was an established business and had a solid fifteen years as a community go-to—beer was piggybacking on the pizza. But, as luck would have it, and unknown to the restaurant owners at the time, a serious hobbyist brewer with a strong desire to brew top-notch English-style ales lived just down the street.

"There was an article in the newspaper," explained Hubert Smith, now in his seventies, who served as the original brewmaster for Wild River from 1990 to 1994. Even before the pizza place had started to brew beer, a local newspaper announced the plans. Smith remembers reading the article: "I shot in there like a bullet," he said.

Just before Thanksgiving 2018, Smith sat down with me at a booth at Wild River Pizza in Grants Pass, one of five of the restaurant's outlets, to reflect on how he arrived at that moment and what brewing skills and knowledge he brought to the pizzeria. He is amiable and good-natured, but he peppers his speech with as many smiles as profanities—and asserts that he is cut from the cloth that makes up the best brewers, stubborn and "pugnacious," although he is far more pleasant than contentious.

Smith had begun homebrewing as a hobby in his years after college. He attended the University of Michigan and, like most from his generation, drank cheap keg beers. "We drank junk beer," he admits. "Just got blasted."

After graduating college in 1960, Smith moved to Ohio to work as a documentary filmmaker, producing educational films. He doesn't recall exactly why, but he picked up homebrewing as a hobby. "Some people like cooking, some people like brewing beer," he explained flippantly.

At the time, homebrewing was still not a sanctioned activity—and Smith had to shop around to find his ingredients and tools. Smith said that he would buy bread yeast and quart tins of malt syrup at the grocery store. "It wasn't very good stuff," he admitted. "People didn't like it much; you know, you'd invite people over [to try it], and after they'd leave, you would look behind your sofa and find they hadn't touched it."

A Pioneering History

For a decade, Smith lived and worked as a documentary filmmaker in Ohio before relocating to Los Angeles. He traveled for what he calls "film gigs," and in 1974, he and his wife spent a year in England—and for the first time, he was exposed to what he says was really good beer. At the time, Campaign for Real Ale had started, an organization decidedly opposed to mass-produced beers and promoted traditional English pub ales. (At the time, Campaign for Real Ale was only a few years old and still a grassroots movement, but it has since grown to nearly 200,000 members.) That year had a profound impact on his appreciation—and understanding—for beers.

After a year in England, Smith returned to LA, where he checked in with the Maltose Falcons, the same group that was lobbying to roll back the restrictions on homebrewing. They provided some tips and feedback and helped Smith improve his beer and brewing techniques.

By the early 1980s, he and his wife were looking for what he called a "lifestyle change," and they moved to Selma, Oregon, "just as the tsunami of hippies was receding," he said, laughing. They bought five acres, a place where they could see the stars at night. Brewing remains a side hobby, but he has become more serious about writing about beer, traveling again to England and to Germany and started judging for the Great American Beer Festival, which began in 1982 with limited competition.

At this point, Smith has been brewing beer for more than twenty years. He likes to talk about "style" versus "fancy," pointing to a blood-orange ale on the menu at Wild River Pizza as something fanciful, something that the brewer does to his fancy, rather than adhering to the classic styles. Smith also seems to draw a hard line between classic and experimentation, placing himself in the former category.

In 1990, when Smith read a newspaper article about a local restaurant, the Wild River Pizza, planning to brew its own beers, he rushed over to tell the owner that he'd brew a batch. "If he doesn't like it, I tell him, 'I'll pay him $100.'" Smith added, "And, if he likes it, 'pay me $100.'"

Over the next four years, Smith was the lead brewer for Wild River Pizza. Somewhat predictably, his style was heavily influenced by classic English ales. In 1992, his Nut Brown Ale

A 1992 silver medal from Great American Beer Festival, the first of many subsequent awards for a southern Oregon beer. *Courtesy of Wild River Pizza.*

won a silver medal at the Great American Beer Festival, only the fifth such honor for an Oregon beer, just two years after Rogue Ale won gold for their Rauch. In the next few years, Smith won three more awards from the Great American Beer Festival for Wild River Pizza—a bronze in the Strong Ale category with a Snug Harbor Old Ale; a bronze for an English-style Bitter; and a silver for a European-style "pilsener."

In 1994, Smith quit. He doesn't remember why. He waved his hand away, as if shooing away the question. He said it had something to do with him being stubborn. He told me that he regrets leaving.

Wild River Pizza has continued to brew its own beer ever since.

6
1996–2014

After the Flood, The Next Chapter Begins

The winter of 1996 in Southern Oregon was a doozy, with heavy snows in the nearby mountains throughout December. And then on New Year's Eve came a double whammy: Temperatures in mountains and higher elevations warmed, and waves of melting snow washed into the valleys; coupled with heavy rains, the rivers and streams swelled more than double and triple their normal size.

Lithia Creek, usually a mellow flatwater stream that rinses from the foothills and trickles through Ashland, suddenly reared up and trounced downtown. Residents were aware that the rains—and possible floods—were coming and had hunkered down with 1,500 sandbags to protect the storefronts and divert any possible flooding. Even so, the water thundered through the plaza like a pack of mad bulls; carrying rocks and tree trunks, the rushing water smashed windows at a local stationery store and pounded through basement businesses like Rogue Ales.

It was the worst flood in decades—and reminiscent of a flood a century earlier, in February 1892, when heavy late winter rains washed through the region, wiping out newly constructed bridges and delaying construction on Medford's first brewery.

As 1997 began, Rogue Ales, located in a beautiful but apparently vulnerable location adjacent to Ashland Creek, was transformed into an aquarium with dirty waist-deep water washing through the entire facility. For two weeks, even the most ambitious businesses in downtown Ashland remained closed as the water supply in town was contaminated and as the town tried to dry out from its aggressive rinse-wash. For Rogue Ales, it was a complete loss, but 90 percent of the beer production had already relocated to its coastal facility in Newport, and this served as a soggy and defeated, but logical, ending. Although Rogue Ales would not reopen its facilities in Ashland, it had already made its contributions to the future of brewing in Southern Oregon by planting a few seeds for the next generation; specifically, two of the brewers from Rogue Ales in Ashland were each poised to start their own breweries.

In fact, by the time the floods ruined the Rogue Ales facility in Ashland, lead brewer Jim Mills had incorporated his new business, Caldera Brewery Co., with the State of Oregon and had plotted his new brewery, not in downtown, but off I-5 Exit 14.

"I was cutting floor drains at the time," said Mills in an interview twenty years later, explaining that he was setting up his brewery (on much higher ground) when the Rogue Ales brewpub was flooded. Over the past two decades, Caldera Brewing has grown steadily into its role as the largest brewery in Southern Oregon. Mills sat across a booth from me in the cavernous dining area for Caldera's brewpub. The ceilings are cathedral-like, sixty feet tall. It was a week before Christmas, and that morning Mills had been out cutting down his family's Christmas tree before rushing into the brewery for our interview. He was friendly and plainspoken, middle-aged but still with a sense of gee-shucks college kid hanging on the edges, as if pulled from central casting, an '80s sitcom dad. He explained that he had started working at Rogue Ales while finishing his college degree at Southern Oregon University.

Mills is exemplary of a new generation of brewers riding a wave that had started in the 1970s with homebrewers and with a couple other emerging trends. Caldera Brewing remains a regional brewery, but it is also knocking at the door for national prominence.

Mills started humbly. He cites his cousin Rick as the initial inspiration.

He grew up in Portland and started college at Montana State, drawn there for the ski team. After his fake ID was taken away, Mills said, he started making his own beer, at first, he said, with kits and extracts, which he admitted weren't very good. Not discouraged by early shortcomings, Mills soon retrofitted his own kit. He was inspired to do better, and soon his beers were popular with his friends.

"My whole inspiration was my cousin Rick," he said, explaining that his older cousin had taken up homebrewing a year after it was legalized, latching on to the new hobby. "I grew up on Henry Weinhards

A Pioneering History

Jim Mills, founder of Caldera Brewing Co. *Author photo.*

and Coors; what my dad was drinking, having sips whenever I could," explained Mills. "Then I tasted my cousin Rick's [beers] and I was totally blown away. They were darker ambers and there was flavor there. It was totally not what I was used to." Mills stood up from the booth where we were talking and ducked into a back office. He returned with a six pack of South Side Ale and another large bottle of a special twenty-year anniversary IPA.

"That's my cousin Rick," he said, pointing to a mug shot photo on the back label. And then he pointed to a skier crouched in a turn, dressed all in dark clothes on the South Side Ale can. "And that's me," he exclaimed.

As a kid, another trend of the late '70s also caught Mills's attention and helped reinforce his interest in what the beer industry could be: In the 1970s, beer can collecting became a popular fad. Like butterfly or stamp collecting, it was a means to preserve and celebrate a disappearing culture—the rarer the can or bottle, the more interesting and valuable.

Mills pointed to the walls above the dining room. The décor in the restaurant is warehouse-chic. Five rows of narrow wood shelves line the circumference of the restaurant walls, probably stretching more than one thousand feet in total and holding several hundred bottles and cans; some say it is the largest collection in the state.

Reportedly the largest beer can and bottle collection in Oregon, located at Caldera Brewing Co. *Author photo.*

Ironically, the epicenter for the beer can collecting fad in the 1970s was none other than St. Louis, home to Anheuser-Busch. In 1970, a local newspaper there profiled a collector, and soon after, other local collectors, who thought they were alone in their particular hobby, connected and together formed the Beer Cans Collectors of America (BCCA)

The fad reached a muted frenzy, with tens of thousands of collectors amassing can collections with the precision of stamp and coin collectors—the older and more obscure the can, the better. At the time, their affection for collecting was in direct opposition to the brewing trends in America, where the number of breweries had dropped to an all-time low of just a few dozen, with 90 percent of the production by a select few breweries, with their millions of mass-produced cans. Membership in BCCA swelled to 11,954 by 1978, and several other associations began; many of the collectors were young boys and teenagers, like Mills at the time.

Mills explained that his collection began when one of his childhood neighbors moved and gave him his bottle collection. It was only a couple dozen bottles at the time, mostly imports, but it sparked something for Mills.

The beer can collecting hobby waned in the early 1980s, but it stuck in the imagination for thousands, like Mills, the idea that a culture of multicolored cans and disparate breweries existed—or even could exist—something different from the monoculture of staid red, white and blue cans of Budweiser or Pabst Blue Ribbon, so ubiquitous and familiar they did not even seem like anything interesting anymore. In part, beer can and bottle collecting crested as a fad because the big breweries soon recognized a market opportunity with the collectors and began issuing their own collector cans; most popularly, St. Paul, Minnesota–based Schmidt Brewery, which was the seventh-largest brewery in the country at the time, began issuing cans with quaint, watercolor images of midwestern wildlife like ducks or deer on a white background. But as the fad was co-opted by the big breweries, it lost that essential element of earnestness and originality that teenage boys and young men seem particularly attuned to, and the fad faded from popularity. At the very same time, though, just as beer can collecting was drifting from popularity, homebrewing was gaining traction. Today, the BCCA still exists, but membership has sunk to a few thousand avid collectors and its membership's average age risen to sixty years old, a solid decade older than Mills.

In 1991, after two years of college in Montana, Mills returned to Oregon to finish his schooling at Southern Oregon University in Ashland—and, importantly, he linked up with a small group of homebrewers, "just five or six guys," he said. The concept for his future brewery began to take shape.

Mills also took a job working in the kitchen at Rogue Ales and soon was volunteering to wash the kegs in the brewery. Four years later, in 1995, he was the head brewer at Rogue Ales in Ashland, but only one-tenth of the beer Rouge Ales was producing was being brewed there; the bulk of the operations had completely relocated to Newport, where it remains today. Also, by the time that Rogue Ales flooded, Mills had already incorporated his own brewery and was building the facility at a site just a football field away from his current, much larger brewery and restaurant.

For the first nine months, he didn't pay himself—and for the next year, only $500 month. Mills explained that when he started Caldera Brewery he would brew for a full day and then distribute kegs from the back of his Subaru for a couple hours in the evening before returning to wash kegs until past midnight, only to wake up at 7:00 a.m. and repeat.

"It was mostly determination," he said. "I had a lot of support, but the determination and drive kept me going—and to see the monthly barrelage go up, and when I could give myself a $200 a month raise, I was super happy."

Those modest days are history. Caldera has moved far past its hand-to-mouth days and far exceeds the capacity and reach for the other breweries in the region, many of which brew only a few tanks, while the facilities at Caldera, in the warehouse attached to the back of the restaurant, holds dozens of tanks. In a single day, Caldera Brewing produces as much beer as Veit Schutz did during an entire year at his City Brewery in Jacksonville, the largest brewery in Southern Oregon in the nineteenth century.

Throughout the brewery, silver tracks flow like a mini roller coaster twisting and turning. Mills explained the different stations for the canning mechanics—where the cans are filled, where they are shuffled side by side and prepared to be linked as a six pack. The brewery has the capacity to can as many as 500 cans per minute. "We're pumping them out pretty quick," Mills admitted. The setup had been owned by Pepsi, Mills explained, hinting at the company Caldera Brewery is now keeping, or at least buying hand-me-downs from.

In fact, these cans—perhaps most well-known is the bright yellow for its IPA—are Caldera Brewery's calling card. For almost the first decade of operations, Caldera Brewing was draft only. But in the early 2000s, Mills received a flier in the mail from a Calgary-based company, the Case Brewing System. It was a typical business-to-business solicitation, and Case was

Caldera was the first craft brewery to sell its beer in cans on the West Coast. *Courtesy of Caldera Brewing Co.*

advertising that it recently had helped the first American craft brewery get its beer into cans.

"At first, I dismissed it," said Mills. At the time, the industry standard was that cans were for the cheap, mass-produced beers like Pabst and Coors. Craft beers wouldn't slum it in cans and were exclusively available on draft or in the more traditional bottles. A couple years earlier, though, in 2002, Oskar Blues Brewery in Colorado started selling its Dale's Pale Ale in cans—and was the first craft brewery in America to do so. Sales grew wildly—and it seemed like it might be the competitive edge that young craft breweries needed.

The craft brewery industry had expanded rapidly in the 1990s after the first generation of homebrewers began opening and operating their own breweries, growing from one to two thousand in less than five years from 1995 to 1999. But the bubble burst by the turn of the twenty-first-century, and over three years, from 1999 to 2002, two hundred breweries closed—a loss of 10 percent of the number of operating breweries. (It would take nearly another decade, until 2008, when the number of breweries once again crested over two thousand.)

The breweries remaining at the start of the twenty-first century were looking for new business equations, new ways to sell the same quality beer, but at lower costs and with wider distribution. In stepped Case Brewing System, first marketing its canning machinery at a Craft Brewers Conference in Cleveland in 2002. It was widely dismissed, but one brewery, Oskar Blues, did take Case up on the idea.

Two years later, Mills made the decision for Caldera Brewing Co. to become the third brewery in America to try out canning for craft beers, and Caldera Brewery was the first on the West Coast to try to sell craft beer in cans.

Mills is plainspoken but precise and insightful about his business and the industry at large. After looking at the flier sent from Case Brewing Systems, he started to break down the cost—and advantages—for distributing in cans. During our interview, he ticked off those reasons: The weight is far less, which means that more volume can be shipped for less, far less. And cans seal better than bottles, decreasing oxidation, which flattens beers' flavors. "It is like a mini-keg," he explained. "It made sense to me, so we jumped in," Mills asserted. He added, "Back then, the only disadvantage was convincing the consumer that you can actually have good beer in a can. Today, there is no disadvantage, except everyone is doing it."

Mills continued, "There was resistance at first. People didn't believe it. We gave out a lot of samples. It was hard because we believed in it, but others didn't yet."

Although sales were initially modest, three years later, Caldera Brewery began adding more of its flavors in cans, including Lawnmower Lager, a smooth, light beer that also had enough heft to please IPA and even stout beer drinkers. Having more than one choice, Mills explained, helped widen the market for them, and soon sales began to shoot upward.

Mills took out a can and pointed to the top rim. "With our can, you can take them anywhere." He pointed to the text running along the upper lip of the can. It reads, "go fishing, go skiing, go boarding, go hike." "That's what we're portraying," he said, "the outdoor lifestyle."

He continued to look at the can, as if seeing it for the first time. Mills is particularly proud of the cans' eye-catching designs—a boldness originally born from a need to grab consumers' attention that has endured. Although Caldera Brewery is a massive operation, with dozens of employees, Mills remains hands-on—and perhaps in no part of the process more than designing the cans.

"It is the favorite part of what I do," he admitted. Mills said he has designed all of the labels himself, even though he has no formal background in design or initially the software to do so. "I couldn't even draw a circle on Adobe when I started," he laughed. Now, he is responsible for almost the entire process from concept to execution—"90 percent," he said. If he hits a snag with technical aspects for designing, Mills works with a friend who is a graphic artist or will YouTube a quick tutorial. It is the same roll-up-your-sleeves elbow grease with which he built Caldera Brewery.

Although originating from the same starting points as Caldera Brewing Co., Southern Oregon's other pioneering brewery, Walkabout Brewery, shares much in its origin story and roll-up-the-sleeves attitude but very little in style or scale. The two breweries began within days of each other, and the brewers at the center for each both were in the same homebrewers group and both worked at Rogue Ales before it left Ashland for Newport.

But Ross Litton is very different from Mills, and each took their breweries in distinct directions, certainly in terms of distribution models—and in the process, showed the spectrum of possibilities for breweries in the region. Litton was from Australia. He had worked as a plumber there but in Oregon did odd jobs, including as a delivery driver and keg cleaner at Rogue Ales.

For the three years before the flood wiped out Rogue Ales, Litton had scrapped for various parts and pieces to cobble together a brewing system.

Cameron Litton hangs out in the brewing room at Walkabout Brewing. *Courtesy of Cameron Litton.*

He cleared out the garage at his family's home at the end of a cul-de-sac in Central Point and set up shop. From a discarded backyard shed, he fabricated a cooler. When a pipe burst, he would cut open a Coke can and cramp it over the leak. It was *Mad Max* style, but it was a functioning seven-barrel system.

Originally, Litton had planned to open a brewpub but abandoned the idea when he considered rent and instead set up the makeshift brewing system in his garage. His original request for a business license befuddled city officials in Central Point. They had never been submitted a request to commercially brew beer in a garage, but a search of local ordinances found nothing to stop him. The brewing system was ad hoc, but it was legally producing top-shelf beers and raking in homebrew awards.

Almost nine months to the day after Rogue Ales flooded and, ultimately, shut down in Ashland, Litton officially opened Walkabout Brewery, within days of Caldera Brewing Co. also opening.

It was the end of the summer, and Litton was thirty-one years old at the time, and his son Cameron, who would take over the business less than two decades later, was just eight years old.

An article in the *Mail Tribune* at that time describes both breweries as planning to produce beers to sell locally. It mentions Walkabout Brewery's flagship beer as Jabberwocky Ale. Meanwhile, Mills was brewing more fanciful "vanilla wheat cream ale, red ale and seasonal beers." Clearly, Mills had not settled into the more traditional, sturdy IPAs and lagers that built his company.

Like Mills driving around to various taverns in the region in his Subaru, Litton also would drive and sell from an aging Honda Civic. In the *Medford Tribune* article, Litton explained, "I can fit six kegs and me in there. The hand truck goes in the trunk, and away we go."

Litton's son, Cameron, also remembers being part of what was packed into the Honda Civic. In an interview on an inky, rainy morning, Cameron recalled growing up with his dad as a minor celebrity and known brewer. But he also distinctly remembers not being overly impressed.

"I wanted nothing to do with my family's thing," he said, matter-of-factly, standing in a room filled with a couple cluttered desks and with the sharp smell of brewing beer. The entire space has several chambers, all connected but distinct—a front room, an office space, the brewing facility in the back and a loading dock with a forklift sitting idle on the side. Adjacent to the other side of the building is a long strip of grassy lawn.

In 2012, Walkabout relocated to this warehouse space in order to expand production and to host its tasting room, which is like a little brother to a brewpub. The Walkabout Brewery warehouse sits in an industrial park in Medford directly across the street from an Anheuser-Busch distribution center as big as an airplane hangar.

"When [the brewery] was at the house, it didn't feel like a real business to me," Cameron admitted. Growing up, his mom worked as a physical therapist and helped keep the family financially afloat during those years, as his dad brewed beer in the garage and drove the family car on delivery runs. Although Cameron grew up around the brewing, helping clean kegs and tanks, he said that he didn't drink at all in high school and, when he left for college, had no intentions to become a brewer or brewery owner.

A Pioneering History

At the University of Oregon, he majored in physical therapy, more closely following his mother's lead, but when he returned to Southern Oregon, he brought back with him schooled management skills and was pulled into the gravitational orbit of Walkabout Brewery.

Like a popular local band that has yet to burst onto a larger stage, Walkabout Brewery has grown a stalwart fan base one drinker at a time—with its patrons adamant that Walkabout Brewery is the best there is and confident that Walkabout Brewery should enjoy further fame and fortune than it currently enjoys. In 2018, for both best brewery and for favorite beer, it handily won the *Rogue Valley Messenger*'s Bestie, a survey of thousands of residents about their favorite foods, drinks and places around Southern Oregon.

At the helm for its popularity is the Workers' Pale Ale, a straightforward beer that rolls with hops. "When it first came out," explained Cameron, "people considered it hoppy. But now they call it malty." He added, "I think it is balanced." The Workers' Pale Ale accounts for more than 80 percent of sales for Walkabout Brewery but really is only one of many. Like a trending band where fans clamor for the most popular song, there is much more in the catalogue to celebrate and explore. The beers at Walkabout Brewery tend to present a heftier profile; notably, sours and pilsners are thin on the lists of beers, if there at all, while sturdier pales, stouts and IPAs tend to make up the starting lineup.

Even so, Cameron believes that loyalty has taken a back seat to experimenting for consumers, as beer drinkers are presented with dozens of new, intriguing options and as the initial generation or two of craft breweries give way to more choices.

Unlike the latter half of the nineteenth century, which primarily offered whatever beer the local brewery cooked up and mostly pulled their flavors from local ingredients, in particular, their choice of hops or, unlike beer through most of the twentieth century, the bulk of which existed in a narrow bandwidth of fizzy pilsners and were mostly differentiated by various marketing campaigns, beer in this segment of the twenty-first century is a matrix of hops, flavor and attitude.

Certainly, some breweries and brewers have their signature styles—like Walkabout Brewery's Workers' Pale Ale—but those are rarely enough to sustain the full attention for a consumer. Not unlike the wide world of current music or movies or TV shows, selection and sensibilities for craft beer seems to be proliferating at lightning speed.

"There's so much good beer out there," said Cameron, "but at the end of the day it is subjective what people like."

Within a twenty-five-mile radius from Medford, there is an entire universe of flavors and styles: In Grants Pass, the Haul is supplied with farmhouse-style beers from Connor Fields Brewing, literally a farmhouse on the outskirts of town; in Medford, Portal Brewery has a selection of stouts and ESPs as wooly as a fisherman's sweater; around the corner from there, Common Block offers more easy-drinking ales and wheat beers; and in Ashland, Standing Stone Brewery prides itself on showing off Oregon's barleys and hops.

The current marketplace for beer is a consumer's paradise of choices and a wide-open expanse for brewers to experiment; but for a business, it is increasingly tricky to establish patrons, especially for the small breweries with little or no budget for marketing. "Everyone is simply taking a smaller piece of pie," Cameron believes.

Although the number of craft breweries has enjoyed double-digit growth over the past decade, the actual amount of craft beer drunk each year has not necessarily kept pace. Americans continue to drink twenty gallons per year, and nationwide that percentage remains about every nine out of ten gallons macro-brewed.

It is a market, though, that does favor nimble breweries like Walkabout Brewery, which can change its offerings in a heartbeat and can experiment with small-batch seasonals and new offerings to tantalize drinkers.

In particular, Cameron is a restless innovator, always looking to push new frontiers. For a while, when IPAs were what everyone was drinking, he actually took them off tap at the tasting room. "It's easy for people to get stuck," he shrugged. "I like to open people's minds."

He is constantly trying new things and new tastes. "I'm always looking for new influences." "If I try a beer I like, we'll all try it," he said, referring to his brewer and staff. "We try to filter out what people are telling us to do and do what we like."

Two beers that are currently on his radar: Boneyard Notorious Triple IPA from Bend, Oregon, and BricktownE Gunslinger, which is as assertive as it sounds, a beer from a downtown Medford brewpub.

Moreover, Cameron is working to keep the branding for Walkabout Brewery relevant and current with the under-thirty-five set, while not alienating the older drinkers who first championed and continue to support the brewery. He has adopted his dad's business and wants to mature it from a pioneer into a more contemporary and competitive brewery.

Cameron is debating changing up the branding that his dad set in place two decades ago, but those alterations present challenges. He wants to honor

A Pioneering History

Taps at Walkabout Brewery. *Author photo.*

his dad's legacy, but he also wants branding to speak to a new generation. It is a dilemma any growing and aging business has, but one particularly keen when locked into family dynamics.

Moreover, sensibilities also have changed since his dad launched the business in the mid-'90s. Walkabout Brewery's icon is the side profile silhouette of a lanky aboriginal man. His dad is from Australia, and the image was meant to honor that heritage but does not necessarily translate to Southern Oregon or, more generally, to present-day political correctness. Cameron has even thought about whether the name Walkabout applies to the brewery anymore, as he was raised in the area, not Australia or somewhere exotic. Ultimately, he said, the name is less about the precise colloquialism—as a "walkabout" references Australians' penchant for extended, wandering journeys and vacations (à la Crocodile Dundee)—but, more generally, can reference an adventurous spirit, universal down under or in Southern Oregon.

"Walkabout is about stepping away," he finally said, explaining that the name will remain the same.

7
NOW AND BEYOND?

By and large, the general rule for business survival is scaling up—and for breweries that means wedging into a market share and expanding distribution. Certainly, it is a business model that serves Caldera Brewing Co. well, with distribution in fifteen states and even in Japan and South Korea. But for the other two dozen or so breweries in Southern Oregon, most survive from a local fanbase and limited territorial range; it is a sensibility at odds with current nationwide trends for breweries and beer. Just like a century earlier, when railroads brought and took boxcars full of ice and refrigerated goods, contemporary distribution of beers is both an import and export business, with craft breweries hoping and needing to establish—and then widen—regional markets, while also fending off competition from the outside.

But Southern Oregon often has not fit comfortably or in step with national trends—and proudly is independent, a trait and attitude that puts most Southern Oregon breweries outside the prevailing conversations about the beer industry.

In general, the overall market for beer is pushed and pulled by a tension between the craft breweries and the giants like Anheuser-Busch, Miller-Coors and Heineken. Of that market, craft beer only accounts for roughly 8 to 10 percent by volume nationwide, a number that continues to expand, but at a rate slower than the growth in the number of microbreweries and brewpubs, meaning each brewery is potentially tapping into a small market segment.

A Pioneering History

Even so, other business metrics provide a wide horizon of optimism. In 2016, craft breweries nationwide produced 24.6 million barrels, which represented a 6 percent rise in volume, but also experienced a promising 10 percent increase in retail dollar value. Furthermore, although only roughly 10 percent of the market share by volume, craft beer represents more than 20 percent market share dollar-wise, meaning the market segment is potentially more valuable.

And the big breweries are recognizing that the craft breweries are nipping at their heels. In response, Anheuser-Busch (a division of global beverage company InBev) has stylized its Super Bowl ads (each thirty-second ad costs as much to air as the entire budget for any of the Medford breweries) to mock small-batch breweries, with taglines like, "not small," "not a hobby," "not a fruit cup" and "not a pony" running over images of their massive, iconic prancing Clydesdale horses. They also have pushed a whole frontier of ads for Bud Light with the slogan, "Bud Light, for the many," and a barrage of pithy ads that ridicule the craft breweries and beer drinkers. In a typical ad, a king walks into a subterranean medieval tavern and announces to a cheering crowd, "Bud Light for everyone." One lone voice, sitting alone in the corner, interjects, "Actually, I'd prefer a nice mead." Somewhat deflated, the king responds, "Bud Lights for everyone… and one mead." Once again, the man injects, "Is it autumnal?" The king flatly announces the order again, "And one autumnal mead." One last time, the man asks, "Is it malty and full-bodied?" The ad ends with the man being clamped into stocks, while the rest of the group cheers.

Behind the scenes, though, InBev is hardly laughing at the micro- and craft breweries—and, instead, has aggressively been gobbling them up where it can. In November 2014, InBev purchased 10 Barrel, a popular Oregon brewery. The flagship 10 Barrel brewpub in Bend was a popular hangout, complete with outdoor firepits and ski chalet motif. The brewery had started less than a decade earlier as a spinoff from a local bar and grill.

For InBev, 10 Barrel is only one of fifteen such acquisitions of popular regional breweries, including Goose Island Beer Co., which was the first brewpub and taproom in Chicago, and Elysian in Seattle, with its tagline "Corporate Beer Still Sucks." More generally, the buying spree by InBev is an acknowledgement that it understands the very real appeal, and threat, from craft beers. Clearly, the King of Beers is rolling out a strategy to buy up and control potentially disruptive competition—not entirely unlike Henry Weinhard purchasing Southern Oregon Brewery in Medford in 1897 when he was trying to expand and control his Oregon fiefdom.

SOUTHERN OREGON BEER

Yet the ecosystem for brewers and beer drinking in Oregon, and especially Southern Oregon, is not necessarily falling under the control of these macro-market forces but remains independent—and potentially even isolated. Consider that while craft beer consumption in the rest of America is 7.8 percent by volume, according to the Oregon Craft Beer site, it is estimated that 53 percent of all draft beer consumed in Oregon is brewed in Oregon, an amount that, sure, includes some bigger breweries like Deschutes in Bend and Full Sail in Hood River, but even so, those breweries are still proudly local and mere drops in buckets like Anheuser-Busch and Miller.

Such statistics certainly indicate an Oregon and, specifically, a Southern Oregon market that favors local production and places like Portal Brewery, which is literally a corner store in downtown Medford.

Like Walkabout Brewery, Portal Brewery also is a family business—and, at its core, has the same charm and the same limitations. The brewery occupies a tight corner space in a century-old historic brick building that, in the past, had been a shed for the city's fire hoses as well as a Red Cross station for soldiers. A small café, it is impossible not to rub elbows with your neighbor there.

Mike Dimon is the brewer, and he learned homebrewing from his grandfather in the late 1970s after it was legalized. His wife, Tessa Delaney, is his business partner, and together they form a quirky and congenial duo. Tessa hand paints growlers with swirling ocean landscapes and whales. (She estimates she has painted one or two thousand growlers, with motifs from the Three Stooges to the *Endless Summer* movie poster to whales swallowing boats.) The list of available beers is presented above the small bar, hand drawn on a chalkboard. With heavy-duty, brain-numbing concoctions like Riptide IPA, Ahab's Hopoon ESB and Hoptopus Imperial Cascadian Dark Ale, the selection nods to the burly and wooly Oregon coast. It is a welcoming and charming pub, but it is unlikely that Portal will ever carve out a bigger slice of the pie.

Hand-painted growlers are part of the charm at Portal Brewery. *Courtesy of Theresa Delaney.*

A Pioneering History

More broadly, that community feeling emanates past the individual brewpubs and throughout the entire universe of Southern Oregon breweries—more chummy than competitive. In 2015, one of the brewers, originally from Wisconsin, formed the Brewery Hockey League, with six breweries on the ice, including Wild River and Walkabout, and in the past, it has included Caldera. They also have spun off a bowling league. And, overarching that community spirit, Medford Beer Week has emerged in recent years as a popular and important kickoff event for Southern Oregon's summer, which includes events all over the city, from cornhole tournaments in alleyways to outdoor movie nights.

Likewise, back at Walkabout Brewing, Cameron is fully on board to use his tasting room as much for beer as a community space, hosting small pop-up concerts and, in the summertime, yoga on the stretch of grass turf adjacent to the brewery—not completely different than the German beer gardens or the Turner Hall at Veit Schutz's City Brewery, which hosted exercise classes on the second floor for the German immigrants in Jacksonville in the 1870s.

"We think of beer as a social connector," said Cameron.

A central question for the future of breweries in Southern Oregon is whether this locally grown, community-oriented business model can sustain two dozen breweries—or, even more ambitiously, if Southern Oregon can provide an earnest and viable countertrend to national trends that are all about size and spread.

Central to that question is whether contemporary breweries can survive without far-reaching distribution like Caldera Brewing. The jury is still out, with evidence on both sides, as Caldera Brewery continues to grow and thrive, but as other local breweries fail to reach the brass ring.

In late summer 2016, Southern Oregon Brewery opened in Medford. The brewery was named for a twice-folded brewery that first launched in 1892, only to be bought up by Weinhard in 1897 and ultimately closed in 1908 with Prohibition. The brewery reopened with local ownership after Prohibition ended in 1933 but closed once again in 1947. In its most recent reincarnation, the brewery was better known as S.O.B. and opened in late 2007, a decade after Caldera Brewing and Walkabout Brewery started the latest generation of breweries in Southern Oregon. Like Caldera Brewing Co., S.O.B.'s aim was to set up a wide-reaching web of distribution, and by 2011, S.O.B. sold almost two thousand barrels throughout Oregon, which placed it in the top quarter of breweries in the state; 23rd largest out of the 110 brewery and brewpubs in Oregon at the time, only 5 percent of its sales happened at the tasting room. But that strategy failed.

In an interview with the *Mail Tribune* shortly before its closure in September 2016, owner Tom Hammond touched on two fundamental shortcomings—S.O.B. failed to elbow its way into an increasingly crowded marketplace throughout the Pacific Northwest, and simultaneously it did not gather up a hometown base.

"The idea of scaling back to be just a local brewery was not a possibility," explained Hammond in his exit interview with the *Mail Tribune*. "Our fixed expense was not compatible with that. We needed to have distribution around the state and the western United States."

But, if family businesses and locally focused brewpubs are, indeed, the present and future for breweries in Southern Oregon, perhaps the polar star for success is Standing Stone Brewery in Ashland. Started in 1997, the year after Walkabout Brewery and Caldera Brewing opened, Standing Stone Brewery was launched by three siblings—and, more than two decades later, remains solid in its popularity, with locals and tourists alike. Just blocks from the Oregon Shakespeare Festival stages, the brewpub overflows during the summer months—and nods toward the clientele with beers like Puck's Porter and The Tempest IPA.

Interestingly, when Standing Stone Brewery opened, it was built around the philosophy of the owners and not built around the brewer, unlike the other two primary breweries at the time, Walkabout in the Medford area and Caldera nearby in Ashland. Also unique, the founders set up a mission statement for the brewery, an approach more common to a nonprofit than a beer business undertaking.

In the mid-1990s, one of the brothers, Emilie Amarotica, saw a note posted on a brick building in downtown Ashland, announcing that the former Pioneer Glass and Cabinet Shop was for sale. The space offered a wide-open warehouse venue, perfect for large brewing tanks (which now sit in the front windows and greet patrons), that reaches out to the Lithia Creek behind the building, where a deck has since been built for summertime visitors. Emilie recruited his two brothers, who were in the Bay Area at the time, Mark and Alex, who had some homebrewing in his background. Hardly cookie-cutter, the brewery is distinctly Southern Oregon, more about community than cash and more about planet than profitability (although they are doing quite fine, thank you). Standing Stone fills its menu with burgers made from local cows and tomatoes and honey from local farms, and it has reduced garbage by 95 percent and has pushed toward zero net energy with solar panels and water recapture. A decade after launching, it was ranked 28th of 100 Best Green Businesses by *Oregon Business Magazine*.

A Pioneering History

Scott Saulsbury, brewer (*left*), and Scott Allen, manager, Standing Stone Brewery. *Author photo.*

With its massive consumption of water and ingredients and packaging, brewing beer is not inherently sustainable, but Standing Stone Brewery has written a different script—and it is one to which other breweries in Southern Oregon are adding.

Caldera Brewing Co., of course, has helped direct an industry change from bottles to cans—and, in the process, dramatically tapped down resource use, both in terms of materials used in packaging and also, with more volume loaded on each truckload, lessened carbon emissions from shipping and transportation. On the coast, near Gold Beach, Arch Rock Brewery hands off its spent grain to the local farmers' cows, and when strip mining threatened local streams, it founded a coalition of craft breweries for clean water, gathering up a dozen regional breweries to aggressively rally lawmakers to set in place protections. And, in downtown Grants Pass, the Haul, a sometimes music venue, is supplied by an off-site brewery, Conner Fields, which operates from a one-hundred-year-old barn in nearby farmland more associated with wine production. The namesake, Jon Conner, is a former sculptor from Brooklyn who ditched the big city for the big open spaces of Southern Oregon—and started making beer. At first, he sold from a stand at the local farmer's market.

With beers balancing classic flavors with a light touch of creativity—like IPL, India Pale Lager and Gold Coast Farm Ale that zings with ginger—its beers announce the flavors of Southern Oregon. Moreover, Conner Fields has plans to plant its own hops fields in the upcoming years, a measure toward reducing the carbon footprint of beer production and also keeping seed-to-sip beer production self-contained in its own ecosystem. If there is a calling card for Southern Oregon breweries, sustainability seems to be an ethic practiced consistently—both for environmental sensibilities and also building strong communities.

In 2016, one of the three brothers from Standing Stone Brewery spun off from the Ashland business and, with his wife, started Common Block Brewery in downtown Medford. There is something that echoes familiar with an earlier era for Southern Oregon, when each small community integrated and supported its own brewery as an integral part of the community and an ad hoc public space. In the past five years, breweries have popped up in small towns like 7 Devils in Coos Bay and, remarkably, two in the coastal town of Brookings, Chetco Brewing Company and Misty Mountain Brewing.

"The location next to Pear Blossom Park is ideal with festivals and happenings in the amphitheater and on the grassy lawn regularly," explained Rachel Koning, marketing and events coordinator for Common Block Brewing, referring to a wide-open, grassy public space adjacent to the public house. "Our covered back patio runs the length of the building and provides a great view of activities across the street. Also, our neighbors across the street, Inn at the Commons, are awesome at sending over large groups staying at the hotel, and we've partnered with them on a Beervana package that includes a night's stay, appetizers and beer at Common Block, and another stop at Portal Brewing Co. for an all-inclusive price."

When Alex and Danielle Amarotico, two of the founders and former owners of Standing Stone Brewery, opened their newest enterprise, once again, they found a historic building to "recycle." A former auto sales room in downtown Medford, the brewpub at Common Block has high ceilings that fill with chatter in the evenings, and outdoor patios bustle with drinkers and dogs during the summer months—a jolt of new life for what has been a sleepy nighttime downtown.

Likewise, as another coda to the turn of the last century, the breweries in Southern Oregon are quite literally connecting to the past. In 2014, a pair of couples in Grants Pass purchased the grand brick building that Marie Kienlen built with her husband in 1902. By Marie's death in 1934, the building had fallen into disuse, and for the next four decades, it was

A Pioneering History

used, in part, as a warehouse for furniture storage. Much like Veit Schutz's City Brewery, what had once been a hub in town was an aging husk of its former self, and by 1973, the owners considered tearing down the former Grants Pass Brewery. But unlike the old brewery in Jacksonville, which was demolished, the former Grants Pass Brewery was rescued from demolition in 1975, renovated to house a restaurant, aptly, but somewhat confusingly, called the Brewery. It has been a well-known establishment for three decades, although, in fact, no beer was actually brewed there until it reopened as Climate City Brewery in 2015.

From the outside, the new brewery looks nearly identical to the brewery one hundred years ago, with the same brick façade facing G Street (formerly Front Street). They no longer draw "artisan water" from the thirty-foot well that had been dug for the original brewery—and for which the site had been chosen—and there are no parrots around, as when Marie walked around the breweries with one perched on each shoulder. The current brewery still draws directly from its history. There is a plaque tucked near the front door announcing "1886 Rogue River Brewery" for the original company that stood at the spot (before being purchased by the Keinlins and before burning down), and the new menus proudly provide a narrative history of the building.

And, as another reference to the building's history and former glory—or perhaps just a fond coincidence—the owners hired a hot shot brewer, a woman who had been brewing at Anderson Valley Brewing in northern California. Although a century has passed since Fredericka Wetterer and Marie Keinlin first owned breweries and helped pioneer the beer industry in Oregon—one hundred years that have included women receiving the right to vote, women CEOs and high-placed politicians—the beer industry itself largely remains a boys' game. But there are exceptions, like Acacia Cooper at Climate City Brewery, who is one of a handful of women brewers in Oregon.

Unlike Fredericka and Marie, though, who worked alone in a man's world, there is now a larger movement connecting women brewers and brewery workers. Started in 2010 by Teri Fahrendorf, a longtime brewer at Steelhead Brewery in Eugene, Pink Boots is a nonprofit with dozens of chapters worldwide and hosts conferences and information exchanges—and, of course, hands out signature knee-high pink boots, perfect for washing tanks and slopping around the brewery floor.

Cooper is eager to talk about her beers and experimentations at Climate City Brewery, but she is humble about the larger significance and about her

Acacia Cooper, Climate City brewer. *Author photo.*

reputation as one of the top brewers in the region, if not the entire Pacific Northwest. She prefers to talk about her choices for new flavors. Three months pregnant and just back from the doctor when she interviewed with me, Cooper admitted that she no longer wears those pink signature boots— "I wore those out," she said—yet, standing on a catwalk between two large brewing tanks and talking confidently about new ideas for new beers, she clearly has one foot in the past and one in the future.

APPENDIX

Current Southern Oregon Breweries

Arch Rock Brewing Company. 28779 Hunter Creek Road, Gold Beach. ArchRockBeer.com
Backside Brewing Co. 1640 NE Odell Avenue, Roseburg.
Bandon Brewing Company & Pizzeria. Bandon.
BricktownE Brewing Company. 44 South Central Avenue, Medford.
Caldera Brewery & Restaurant. 590 Clover Lane, Ashland. CalderaBrewing.com
Chetco Brewing Company. 830 Railroad Street, Brookings. ChetcoBrew.com
Climate City Brewing Company. 509 SW G Street, Grants Pass. ClimateCityBrewing.com
Common Block Brewing Company. 315 East Fifth Street, Medford. CommonBlockBrewing.com
Conner Fields Brewing. 121 SW H Street, Grants Pass.
Klamath Basin Brewing Company. 1320 Main Street, Klamath Falls. KBBrewing.com
Old 99 Brewing Co. 3750 Hooker Road A, Roseburg. Old99Brewing.com
Opposition Brewing Company. 545 Rossanley Drive, Medford. OppositionBrewing.com
Osmo's Alehouse. 522 South Central Avenue, Medford.
Portal Brewing. 100 East Sixth Street, Medford.
7 Devils Brewing Co. 247 South Second Street, Coos Bay. 7DevilsBrewery.com
Standing Stone Brewing Company. 101 Oak Street, Ashland. StandingStoneBrewing.com

Appendix

Two-Shy Brewing. 1308 NW Park Street, Roseburg. TwoShyBrewing.com
Vice Brewing Company. 220 SW H Street, Unit A, Grants Pass.
Walkabout Brewing Co. 921 Mason Way, Medford. WalkaboutBrewing.com
Wild River Brewing & Pizza Co. 595 NE E Street, Grants Pass. WildRiverBrewing.com

BIBLIOGRAPHY

Articles

Buckingham, Lucy. "Mapping Beervana." *Portland Monthly* (July 2013).
Central Point American. "The Days of Yore." February 23, 1933.
Darling, John. "Oregon's Long Brewing History on Tap." *Medford Mail Tribune*, September 20, 2016.
Duewel, Jeff. "Beer by the Bucketful." *Daily Courier*, February 2003.
Kalp, Randy, and Bethany Salvon. "Why Southern Oregon Is America's Next Beer Capital." *Condé Nast Traveler*, November 27, 2014.
Kettler, Bill. "Now Brewing by the Barrel." *Mail Tribune*. September 5, 1997.
Messer, Ryan. "Bert Grant: The Godfather of Craft Brewing." *Yakima Magazine*, June 23, 2017.
Smith, Hubert. "Ancient Ales and Later Lagers: Beer Wars of Early Oregon." *Table Rock Sentinel* (January–February 1991).
Woodward, Bob, and Laurel Bermen. "Oregon Beer History: The Brave History of Brewing's Triumph Over Time." *1859 Magazine* (September 2009).

Blogs

OldBreweries.com
OregonBrewLab.com
Wikipedia.org

BIBLIOGRAPHY

Books

Dodge, Orvil. *Pioneer History of Coos and Curry Counties: Heroic Deeds and Thrilling Adventures of the Early Settlers.* Salem, OR: Capital Printing, 1898.
Dunlop, Pete. *Portland Beer: Crafting the Road to Beervana.* Charleston, SC: The History Press, 2013.
History of Southern Oregon, Comprising Jackson, Josephine, Douglas, Curry and Coos Counties. Portland, OR: A.G. Wallings, 1884.
Meier, Gary, and Gloria Meier. *Brewed in the Pacific Northwest: A History of Beer Making in Oregon and Washington.* Seattle, WA: Fjord Press, 1991.

Historical Collections

"Digging for Gold Created a Mighty Thirst." Jacksonville Booster Club and Woodlands Association, placard at site of old brewery.
Historical Oregon Newspapers, oregonnews.uoregon.edu.
Josephine County Historical Society, folders on Grants Pass Brewery, photos by Marie Keilen.
Southern Oregon Historical Society, folders on Veit Schutz, Joseph Wetterer, Fredericka Wetterer.
Southern Oregon History Revised, curated by Ben Truwe, truwe.sohs.org.
200 Years of Oregon Beer. Oregon Historical Society exhibit, October 2018.

Interviews

Allen, Scott, general manager, Standing Stone. Personal interview, November 27, 2018.
Cooper, Acacia, head brewer, Climate City Brewery. Personal interview, November 28, 2018.
Delaney, Tessa, owner, Portal Brewing. Email correspondence. November 22–25, 2018.
Edmunson-Morton, Tiah, curator. Oregon Hops and Brewing Archives. Personal interview, December 5, 2018.
Ellis, Nick, owner, Opposition Brewery. Personal interview, November 26, 2018.
Litton, Cameron, owner, Walkabout Brewery. Personal interview, November 26, 2018.

BIBLIOGRAPHY

Mills, Jim. Founder, Caldera Brewing Company. Personal interview, December 13, 2018.

Smith, Smith, former brewer, Wild River Pizza. Personal interview, November 26, 2018.

Presentations

Jacksonville Historical Walk, conducted by Carolyn Kingsworth, October 28, 2018.

Oregon Public Broadcasting. *Beervana* (Oregon Experience Documentary) Beth Harrington, producer/writer, 2007.

"When All the World Was Young: The Coming of the Railroad to Southern Oregon" (script for PowerPoint presentation). Larry Mullaly, 2009.

ABOUT THE AUTHOR

Phil Busse is a Wisconsin-raised and Oregon-based writer. He has done his tour of duty with alt-weeklies. After graduating from Middlebury College in Vermont, he hightailed it to the West Coast, where he started his writing career with *San Francisco Weekly*. During law school at the University of Oregon, he followed a crime beat for *Eugene Weekly* and, in 2000, helped start the *Portland Mercury*, serving as the publication's managing editor for the first five years. Phil serves as the executive director for the Media Institute for Social Change (MediaMakingChange.org), an educational nonprofit he launched in 2006, and he is the publisher and editor for the *Rogue Valley Messenger*, a newspaper he helped start in 2014 to bring news, entertainment and, yes, beer reviews to Southern Oregon.